To my good f[...]

Baird on her [...]

Petunia, Celestial Rose

# ANNUALS FOR YOUR GARDEN

GIANT IMPERIAL LARKSPURS

[2]

# ANNUALS
## FOR YOUR GARDEN

BY

DANIEL J. FOLEY

NEW YORK
THE MACMILLAN COMPANY
1938

Typography and Illustrations by

J. HORACE MCFARLAND COMPANY
*Mount Pleasant Press*
HARRISBURG, PENNSYLVANIA

# Author's Note

GLANCING over the proofs of this little book, I am reminded of the limitations imposed by the space of 96 pages, and regret the enforced exclusion of certain of the lesser-known Annuals. Nevertheless, the ninety genera treated present a representative collection of Annuals for the small home-garden. Indeed, few amateurs, and certainly no beginner, would attempt to grow in one season all the varieties discussed. Assuredly, pleasant surprises await those gardeners who, after gaining experience with the more familiar Annuals, are willing each year to try a few of the more unusual kinds.

It is for the beginner, in particular, that these pages have been written. Having grown up in a garden, I know something of the problems that confront new enthusiasts, not the least of which are the botanical names and their pronunciation. With this in mind, a simple guide to pronunciation has been included. It must not be considered infallible; unfortunately, there is no commonly accepted standard among gardeners. In any event, it is earnestly hoped that the tyro with Annuals will not confine his efforts to those with "easy" names, and thus overlook many garden treasures.

It is hardly necessary to mention the great enthusiasm for gardening now being manifested in all parts of our country. In writing "Annuals for Your Garden," I have merely attempted to make suggestions for the more complete enjoyment of your hobby and mine.

# ACKNOWLEDGMENTS

I wish to acknowledge the courtesy of the following firms whose coöperation has made possible the use of many of the color plates in this book.

JOSEPH BRECK & SONS, Boston, Mass.
H. G. HASTINGS Co., Atlanta, Ga.
ARTHUR LEE, Bridgeport, Pa.
HENRY F. MICHELL COMPANY, Philadelphia, Pa.
WALTER S. SCHELL, INC., Harrisburg, Pa.
MAX SCHLING SEEDSMEN, INC., New York, N. Y.
STEELE, BRIGGS SEED Co., LTD., Toronto, Canada
STUMPP & WALTER Co., New York, N. Y.

In preparing this little book, I have had the valuable guidance of Dr. J. Horace McFarland, and the helpful assistance of my associates at the Mount Pleasant Press. To all of them I am most grateful.

DANIEL J. FOLEY

*Harrisburg, Pa.*
*March 1, 1938*

# Annuals in the Landscape

EACH YEAR, with the approach of spring, new groups of enthusiastic beginners turn their attention to the making of a garden. As with many hobbies, these novices, fired with fresh hope, anticipate the living pictures which they are ambitious to create. Observation has taught them that pictures or vistas of everchanging beauty are possible in the average back yard. To be sure, effort is involved, but that neither baffles nor disturbs the optimism of these beginners. Usually little consideration is given to a definite plan; rather, the plants are set in beds or borders or in rows. It is only after a year or two of experience that beginners give thought to the design or pattern of their garden plots.

In a general way, garden designs may be classified as formal or informal. Formal areas are planned on the basis of symmetrical balance, using a rectangular, a circular, a square pattern, or any of the deviations of these forms. To unify the design, a terminal or a central feature is used. It may be a sundial, a bird-bath, a gazing-globe, a bench, a fountain, a specimen plant, a piece of statuary, a pergola, or some other object introduced to create or to accentuate the desired unity. The annual plants selected are usually grouped in beds to provide the color, the form, and the texture of the everchanging picture the gardener is attempting to create.

In contrast to the straight lines and sharp angles of formal gardens, undulating curves make the characteristic outlines of informal gardens. Balance is usually obtained with irregular foliage masses placed in a more natural relation than the symmetrical arrangement usually found in formal gardens. The features used in formal areas have their place in this type of garden, but they need to be utilized with discretion.

After all, the beauty of the average home-garden is created by an appropriate selection and a pleasing association of plant materials.

Indeed, it may be said that color, form, and texture are the dominant features in any landscape vista. Generally speaking, *color* has a stronger appeal to the imagination than either form or texture. There is something about the tints and the shades in nature that fascinates us. As we glance out over a landscape for the second time, we are made conscious of the *forms* that make up the pictures. Most of the forms we see in nature can be reduced to simple geometrical designs. It is the endless variety of combinations within these designs that gives gardening its tremendous appeal. Then as we become more familiar with plants, we realize the importance of *texture* in the landscape. It may be that the growth is strong and coarse, or delicate and lacy.

In any event it is these three distinguishing characteristics that we find in the landscape, and we do well, usually, when they are the features we intelligently strive for in our gardens.

Annuals are those plants which complete their life-cycle in one growing season, and they can be utilized to great advantage in almost every garden. They are practically indispensable for your garden and mine because of their adaptability, their freedom of bloom, and their rapidity of growth, as well as their inexpensiveness.

It matters not whether annuals are grown in a garden of formal design, in a rock-garden, in the perennial or shrub-border, in a cutting garden, or in window-boxes. Indeed, they may be used to advantage to border vegetable gardens, to adorn public parks, as well as to provide a homelike feeling about summer residences.

Annuals offer unlimited opportunities for immediate landscape effects, in addition to providing quantities of desirable cut-flower material. As such they may be esteemed an almost vital part of our garden picture; their short life-span provides opportunity for meeting garden necessities akin to emergencies.

# Starting Annuals from Seed

AMONG the Annuals there are three distinct groups: *Tender* Annuals are those plants which by their very nature and requirements will not bloom outdoors in northern sections unless they have been started in a greenhouse or coldframe. Requiring a longer period of development before flowering than could be had if sown in the open ground, plants like Scarlet Sage would be unable to complete their cycle before frost. *Half-hardy* Annuals are those plants which can endure little lowering of temperature, and, like Tender Annuals, must not be set out until all danger of frost is past. *Hardy* Annuals, like Bachelor Buttons and Annual Larkspur, may be sown directly in the open ground; oftentimes better results are obtained when the seed is sown in the fall.

Certain Perennials, like Snapdragons, and Biennials, like Salvia farinacea, which bloom the first year from seed, are treated as Annuals because they are best adapted as such in many regions.

It is hardly necessary to say that only the best quality of seed should be used. Many seedsmen have given close attention to the improvement of particular strains and varieties of Annuals, with the result that amateurs can now obtain seeds of really superior quality from the reputable seedsmen.

Seed sown indoors may be planted either in seed-pans or in flats. Small flats about the size of a cigar-box are very convenient for the average gardener. Shallow clay pots of varying sizes are useful for small quantities of seed. They are easy to handle in the home. Whenever possible it is better to get new pots; if old ones are used, scour them thoroughly to destroy any fungus spores that may have established themselves in the porous clay. For the same reason, clean all flats thoroughly.

*Drainage* is the first consideration. Bore holes in the bottoms of the wooden flats, or provide for spaces between the boards when constructing the seed-boxes. Use a layer of gravel, cinders, or pieces of broken flower-pots above the outlets in pots.

Amateurs will find that well-sifted soil, composed of equal

parts of loam, sand, and leaf-mold, is the most satisfactory medium for starting seed. The use of fertilizer is not advisable.

Having provided for drainage, fill the receptacle with the soil-mixture, and tamp lightly but firmly. A space of approximately one-half inch between the level of the soil and the top of the flat provides for watering. To conserve space and facilitate transplanting, sow seed in rows. However, fine seed should be mixed with sand, and, if sown in small quantities, may be scattered broadcast. Sieve sand or finely screened soil to merely cover the seed. Large seeds are generally covered to a depth of three times their diameter; small seeds are given only enough covering to keep them moist; or, better still, merely press them into the soil. In any event, make the surface of the seed-pan or flat level, to allow for even watering.

*Watering* is of vital importance. A piece of moist burlap, placed over the seed-flat, will prevent seed from being washed away. Even if this measure is not taken, water should always be applied through a fine spray nozzle. Sprinkling-cans with fine spray nozzles are easily obtained. For very small seed use an atomizer in watering. Some gardeners prefer to set seed-pans in water, allowing the water to seep in through the drainage-holes until the surface of the soil is moist. This method is most satisfactory; the moisture is evenly distributed and the seed is not disturbed. Since the seed must not be allowed to dry out nor the soil to become soggy, a moist condition may be maintained by covering the pans with paper or glass, or both. When moisture collects on the glass, take it off carefully, and remove all covering when seedlings break through the soil.

Not infrequently during rainy spells, "damping off," caused by an annoying fungus, occurs in hotbeds, coldframes, and greenhouses. The thread-like structure of the fungus spreads rapidly over the surface of the soil, causing the seedlings to wilt. A high degree of humidity seems to encourage the development of this fungus; hence watering should be done in the morning when air is allowed to circulate more freely in the greenhouse or home. An organic mercury compound known as Semesan, or a solution of potassium permanganate, may be used to check this fungus. Some people find it desirable to sterilize their soil and seeds with Semesan before planting.

Many gardeners allow seedlings to develop eight or more leaves before transplanting, with the result that spindly growth is produced. Unless the seedlings are too small to handle conveniently, they should be transplanted when the first pair of true leaves have developed. (If growing annuals which resent transplanting, use individual clay, fiber, or paper pots.)

As the seedlings assume their growth habit, it will be found that they tend to become spindly. Pinching out the top of the main stem will check the top-growth and help to develop a stronger root-system as well as to produce a bushy plant.

ACROCLINIUM HYBRIDS
*See page 17*

In planting annuals where they are to grow and bloom, one should realize that well-prepared, fertilized soil usually gives best results. Preparation should take place several weeks before planting; fresh manure needs to be dug in during the fall. To be sure, some annuals grow well in poor soil, or rather are hastened into bloom with scant fertility. However, plant-food, either chemical or fibrous, is generally essential in preparing the annual garden, and applications of liquid manure at intervals throughout the season will prove helpful.

Perhaps the most neglected part of maintenance is the job of staking. Some plants by the very nature of their growth demand this attention, while others are greatly improved and give the garden a tidy appearance if stakes are used. Do not wait until wind and rain have laid low your choice annuals; stake your plants while they are straight and easy to handle.

Annuals respond readily to moisture. It is far better to water the garden thoroughly once a week than to give the sur-

AGERATUM, BLUE BOY
*See page 17*

[ 12 ]

SNAPDRAGON (ANTIRRHINUM) HYBRIDS
*See page 20*

face of the ground a sprinkling every day. In areas where water is at a premium, the garden must rely on nature, cultivation, and the use of mulches.

Insects and plant diseases often give us more concern than we anticipate. However, there are many standard kinds of insecticides and poisons available. To counteract all sucking insects like aphids (usually found on the under surface of the foliage or flowers or along the stems of plants), use a contact insecticide containing nicotine or pyrethrum. Chewing insects like beetles and cutworms are best defeated by using a stomach poison like arsenate of lead. Poison bait is often used to control cutworms, but it is best to kill them by hand-picking.

# The All-America Selections

SINCE 1932, progressive American seedsmen have been featuring new plants selected by the All-America Council, sponsored by the Southern Seedsmen's Association and the American Seed Trade Association.

The purpose of this organization is set forth here by the Chairman, W. Ray Hastings:

"The Council is acting as Official Registrar of new varieties, flowers and vegetables, commonly propagated by seed. It endeavors to obtain all new varieties believed to be worthy, from anywhere in the world, the season before proposed introduction. In twelve different locations in America, trials of these flowers and vegetables are run in open-field competition. From these trials, entered under genus and number only, the judges determine what varieties might be recommended by the Seed Trade and featured to the gardeners of America."

The awards given are designated as follows:

G. M., Gold Medal; A. M., Award of Merit; H. M., Honorable (Special) Mention.

Much confusion and duplication have been avoided and confidence has been stimulated by the careful awards of the All-America Council. These have included the following items:

ANCHUSA, Bluebird. H. M., 1935.

ANTIRRHINUM, Celestial. A. M., 1938.
Royal Rose. H. M., 1936.
St. George. H. M., 1936.
Rustproof, University of California Mixture. Award of Horticultural Achievement, 1935.
Rust-resistant, White Spire. H. M., 1937.

ASTER, CHINA, El Monte. H. M., 1936.
Los Angeles. A. M., 1934.
Silvery Rose. H. M., 1934.
Wilt-resistant Strains. Special Award of Horticultural Achievement, 1933.

CALENDULA, Orange Fantasy. A. M., 1938.
Orange Shaggy. G. M., 1935.
Sunshine or Chrysantha. G. M., 1934.

CALLIOPSIS, Golden Crown. A. M., 1938.

CANTERBURY BELL, Angelus Bell. H. M., 1934.
Annual Mixed. G. M., 1933.
Liberty Bell. A. M., 1934.

CELOSIA, Flame of Fire. H. M., 1935.

CHRYSANTHEMUM, Eldorado. H. M., 1934.

CORNFLOWER (Centaurea), Jubilee Gem. A. M., 1937.

[ 15 ]

CALIFORNIA SUNSHINE ASTERS
*See page 31*

Cosmos, Orange Flare. G. M., 1935.
Sensation, Mixed. A. M., 1936.
DELPHINIUM, Cambridge Blue.
A. M., 1933.
DIANTHUS LACINIATUS SPLENDENS.
H. M., 1935.
HUNNEMANNIA, Sunlite. A. M., 1934.
LARKSPUR, Blue Bell. H. M., 1934.
Rosamond. G. M., 1934.
White King. H. M., 1937.
LINARIA, Fairy Bouquet. G. M.,
1934.
LUPINE, Giant King, Mixed. A. M.,
1933.
MARIGOLD, Crown of Gold. G. M.,
1937.
Dwarf Royal Scot Alldouble.
H. M., 1937.
Guinea Gold. G. M., 1933.
Golden Beauty. H. M., 1935.
Dixie Sunshine. A. M., 1936.
Monarch, Mixed. A. M., 1934.
Primrose Queen. H. M., 1935.
Yellow Beauty. H. M., 1935.
Yellow Supreme. G. M., 1935.
NASTURTIUM, Golden Gleam. G. M.,
1933.
Glorious Gleam Hybrids. A. M.,
1935.
Golden Globe. A. M., 1936.
Scarlet Gleam. G. M., 1935.
PANSY, Coronation Gold. A. M.,
1938.
Dwarf Swiss Giants. A. M., 1933.

POPPY, Iceland, Yellow Wonder.
H. M., 1937.
PETUNIA, Burgundy. H. M., 1937.
Dainty Lady. A. M., 1936.
Flaming Velvet. G. M., 1936.
Gaiety. H. M., 1938.
Improved Rose King. H. M.,
1936.
Martha Washington. A. M., 1935.
Orchid Beauty. A. M., 1938.
Pink Gem. G. M., 1934.
Rose Gem. A. M., 1936.
Salmon Supreme. A. M., 1938.
Topaz Rose. H. M., 1938.
Victorious, Mixed. A. M., 1934.
PHLOX, Gigantea Art Shades. A. M.,
1935.
SCABIOSA, Giant Hybrids, Mixed.
H. M., 1934.
STOCK, Giant Excelsior, Rose-Pink.
H. M., 1937.
VENIDIUM FASTUOSUM. A. M., 1933.
VERBENA, Beauty of Oxford Hy-
brids. A. M., 1933.
Cerise Queen. H. M., 1934.
Dannebrog. A. M., 1934.
Floradale Beauty. A. M., 1937.
Lavender Glory. A. M., 1933.
Spectrum Red. H. M., 1934.
Violet Bouquet. H. M., 1935.
ZINNIA, Fantasy, Mixture. A. M.,
1935.
Fantasy, Star Dust. A. M.,
1937.

# Worthwhile Annuals

ACROCLINIUM (ak-roh-klyn'i-um). EVERLASTING

This unassuming little plant from Australia has evidently given the botanists a headache. It is more properly known as Helipterum, and includes a pleasing species of everlasting which is sometimes listed as Rhodanthe. In recent years, Acroclinium has had the attention of the hybridizers, with the result that a remarkable strain of rich rose-pink flowers on fifteen-inch stems is now available. (See illustration on page 11.) An arrangement of the blossoms in varying stages of development makes a most effective display. Their straw-like character brings to mind their most popular use—as everlastings.

Sow the seed in the open ground and set the plants four to six inches apart in full sun. Acroclinium roseum is best grown in rows in the cutting garden. Seed may be sown at intervals of two weeks if a large quantity of flowers is desired. For winter bouquets, cut the blooms before they have opened fully, and remove the foliage. Then hang them to dry in a dark place with their heads down.

AGERATUM (a-jer-ay'tum or ah-jer'ah-tum). AGERATUM

Blue flowers have a universal appeal, and not the least popular is the Ageratum. Today we associate the name with several dwarf forms which are most useful for bedding and edging in the garden. In recent years, many amateurs have made cuttings from their choicest plants in the fall in order to grow Ageratum in their window gardens. The fluffy texture of the flower-heads, together with the hairy or pubescent character of the foliage, the rich blue color, and the compactness of form are the distinguishing characteristics of this most desirable plant, which is native in tropical America. Although the familiar garden form, which makes an excellent cut-flower, reaches a height of eighteen inches or more, the improved varieties are seldom more than six to nine inches in height. (See illustration on page 12.)

For early bloom seed must be started indoors, and it is well to remember that plants of soft, succulent growth are easily nipped by late spring frost.

[ 17 ]

Hence the young plants should not be set out until the ground is warm, at which time seed may be sown out-of-doors for fall blooming. Where very formal edging effects are desired, it is best to propagate all plants from cuttings to assure uniformity of height and color. (Always grow a few extra plants to replace losses by disease or drought.) Watering thoroughly, and removal of all dead flowers and diseased plants are the essential factors for the maintenance of an edging of Ageratum.

## ALTHÆA (al-thee'a). HOLLYHOCK

Reminiscent of simple cottages and deserted farmhouses, the stately Hollyhocks seem to be a cherished bit of old-time grace revived in modern gardens. Seldom do we use the botanical name, Althæa, which is the Greek equivalent of Marsh Mallow. Hollyhocks are best treated as biennials, but sometimes they carry over for several winters. In recent years, an improved strain, blooming the first year from seed, has been developed. For immediate background effects or for accent purposes, these annual kinds are useful, since they grow four feet tall or more.

Sow the seed during February or early March in a sunny window, a greenhouse, or a coldframe. Since the plants have long tap-roots, the seedlings should be transplanted to their permanent places as soon as four leaves have formed. If this is not possible, place them in small pots for later transplanting to the garden.

## ALYSSUM, SWEET (a-liss'um). SWEET ALYSSUM

In the Middle Ages, when men depended largely on plants for medicine, Alyssum came to be known as Madwort because it was believed to help one overcome anger. Perennial species, like A. saxatile and A. rostratum, are widely used in rock-gardens and perennial borders. The annual species we call Sweet Alyssum (A. maritimum) is classified by botanists as Lobularia maritima (a name which is seldom used). In masses, for edging purposes, or as a filler in the rock-garden, this annual is invariably successful.

White flowers are essential in any well-balanced garden, and edgings of plants like Sweet Alyssum help to unify flower-beds and lawn areas. Little Gem, a compact white form; Lilac Queen, with its lilac-tinted blossoms, and the double-flowering form often grown in greenhouses are familiar to almost every gardener. Then too, many seed-houses offer selected, new, dwarfer and more compact forms which should not be overlooked.

A hardy annual which frequently sows itself, Alyssum blooms in six weeks from seed, which may be planted directly in the open ground. If sown thinly, it will not be necessary to transplant. Frequent shearing stimulates new growth and a succession of bloom.

## AMARANTHUS (am-a-ran'thus). AMARANTH

This rather coarse-looking foliage plant is one of the most brilliantly colored annuals grown in American gardens. Its botanical name refers to the lasting character of the flowers, which are often dried for use in winter bouquets. Amaranthus caudatus, known as Love-lies-bleeding, has long, pendulous racemes of deep red flowers, on three to four-foot stems. Several kinds, averaging two to three feet, with brilliant red and multicolored foliage, are classed as forms of A. tricolor; among them are Joseph's Coat, Molten Fire, and Sunrise.

Amaranthus grows easily from seed and thrives in soil that is low in fertility. Sow the seed in a coldframe or in the open ground and set the plants at least twelve inches apart in full sun.

## AMMOBIUM (am-moe'bi-um). WINGED EVERLASTING

A Greek name which presumably refers to its native Australian habitat, "living in sand," is attached to this annual. The common name, Winged Everlasting, is derived from the curious winged character of the stems. In rich soil, the plants often grow three feet tall. The rather modernistic angular stems support clusters of white papery flowers marked with yellow centers.

Seed may be sown out-of-doors and the plants set in full sun at least nine inches apart. If one wishes to use the flowers for winter bouquets, they should be cut before they are fully opened and hung to dry, heads down.

## ANAGALLIS (a-na-gal'lis). PIMPERNEL

Known also as Poor Man's Weatherglass, Anagallis, the Greek for "delightful," is all that its name implies. Yet it is too little grown and appreciated. The brilliant blue and scarlet

[ 19 ]

kinds are delightful for miniature arrangements. Bluebird, a hybrid of Anagallis arvensis, is valuable for the note of blue it gives to the summer garden, replacing the dainty Aubrietias of spring. As with many annuals, a packet of mixed seed always offers surprises to the amateur because of the unusual color effects that are obtainable. Anagallis fits well into the rock-garden, or it may be used as a border plant. A. arvensis grows four to six inches, and A. grandiflora is somewhat taller.

Sow the seed in the open ground, preferably in a sunny spot. Anagallis requires little care except where it may tend to self-sow and become something of a weed, though an agreeable one.

## ANCHUSA (an-koo'sa). BUGLOSS

Better known as Bugloss or Alkanet, Anchusa, which in Greek means "a paint for the skin" or "a rouge," is generally treated as a perennial. A. italica, Dropmore is the tall-growing perennial form often seen in gardens, and A. capensis is a more compact biennial kind. In the 1935 All-America Selections, an annual form of A. capensis known as Bluebird was given Honorable Mention. The plant is compact, seldom more than eighteen inches tall. Its rich indigo-blue flowers are borne in generous clusters above the noticeably pubescent foliage which is characteristic of the genus. There are few other flowering annuals of a richer blue tone than Anchusa, Bluebird.

Sow the seed in a coldframe and set the plants nine inches apart in full sun. Rich soil benefits all the species of this genus. Use it in masses for foreground plantings as a companion to the orange or lemon Calendulas.

## ANTIRRHINUM (an-tir-ry'num). SNAPDRAGON

This Greek name for the familiar Snapdragon, which is native to the warm climate of the Mediterranean, means "nose-like," in reference to the form of the flowers and seed-pods. In Shake-speare's time, Snapdragons were highly cherished in gardens. For generations in England they have been associated especially with wall-gardens. Although perennials in their native habitat, these showy plants are treated as hardy annuals in our gardens, where they often self-sow. In mild parts of the eastern United States, from Philadelphia southward, old plants sometimes live over winter. Truly magnificent in their color-range, the many recently improved varieties of Antirrhinum are valued for cutting, for bedding, or for bright masses in many parts of the garden, as well as for edging purposes. (See illustration on page 13.)

The types may be grouped according to height. Maximum or Super-Giant kinds often exceed three feet in height, but always require staking. For garden use, the Majus types, averaging two to two and one-half feet, are most suitable, but they too need support. The Nanum Grandiflorum types, twelve to eighteen inches in height, make effective masses in small areas and are best suited to the average garden. Among the novelties are the "Midget" Antirrhinums which are seldom more than six inches tall and are desirable for rock-gardens. Pure white, many shades of pink, rose, red, orange and yellow, some of which are pastel tints and others of definitely brilliant hues, are obtainable in the hundred or more named varieties of the types mentioned above.

For midsummer bloom, the seed is best started indoors or in a coldframe. When planning to grow Snapdragons in quantity, it is best to buy separate colors. Pinch the centers of the seedlings and set them in rich garden soil. Determine the space between plants by the height of the particular strain; usually the distance between plants is equal to one-half the maximum height. Snapdragons will bloom freely as long as seed-pods are not allowed to develop. The occurrence in recent years of a rust disease almost put an end to these sturdy annuals for garden use, but through recent research and selection, rust-resistant strains are now available, and it is advisable to buy only these strains. Diseased plants should always be destroyed.

## ARCTOTIS (ark-toe′tis). African Daisy

This name is the Greek for "bear's ear," a reference to the botanical structure of the seeds, but the familiar name, Blue-eyed African Daisy, is more descriptive. Related to the great family of Composites, this South African genus contains several desirable species for American gardens.

Arctotis breviscapa is compact in form, grows six inches tall, and is literally covered with brilliant orange flowers accentuated with dark centers. It prefers full sun and a sandy location, and may well be called a dramatic annual, so intense is its color. Decidedly more subdued in its coloring is the Blue-eyed African Daisy, A. grandis or A. stœchadifolia. A vigorous grower, often two and one-half feet tall, the grayish white flowers are banded with blue, which blends well with the adjoining zone of soft yellow. These blue daisies are flowers of great beauty in the sunlight, but close in the late afternoon. The plants bloom over a long period.

Sow the seed in a coldframe or in the open ground. Set the seedlings of A. breviscapa four to six inches apart, and those of A. grandis twelve inches apart. Sandy soil and full sun are their only requirements.

## ARGEMONE (are-jem'o-nee). PRICKLY POPPY

The derivation of this Greek name, which refers to an eye disease believed to have been cured by this plant, brings to mind the curious herbals of the sixteenth and seventeenth centuries. At that time "vertues" were ascribed to practically all the plants in cultivation, and among them was Argemone mexicana, the Mexican Prickly Poppy. It is an unusually decorative plant in the garden, especially when it sows itself and comes up at random. The large, white, cup-shaped flowers, held on stiff stems, and the glaucous, white-veined, spiny foliage suggest the hot sandy regions of Mexico, where this plant is found naturally.

Sow the seed in the open ground, scattering it in hot, sunny areas where tall plants (three to four feet) are needed. While it is difficult to transplant the seedlings, some gardeners are successful. If you must transplant it, move it with a ball of earth, or start the plants in small pots.

## ASTER, CHINA. See Callistephus, page 27.

## BALSAM. See Impatiens, page 54.

## BRACHYCOME (bra-kick'o-me). SWAN RIVER DAISY

The Swan River Daisy is one of the pleasing annuals we owe to far-away Australia. Brachycome is the Greek for "short hair" in reference to the seed-vessels. Its tiny daisy-like blossoms are borne on slender stems, which are most desirable for miniature bouquets. The available colors of B. iberidifolia are purple, blue, pale lilac, rose, and white. In the rock-garden, as edging plants, or in masses these twelve-inch plants are most effective.

Sow the seed in a coldframe or in the open ground and set the plants

CALENDULA CHRYSANTHA OR SUNSHINE
*See page 26*

**CALLIOPSIS, GOLDEN CREST**
*See page 27*

four to six inches apart. It is hardly advisable to set them in single rows, even for borders; they are much more effective in wide edgings. Pinch back the young plants and set them in full sun to develop sturdy growth.

## BROWALLIA (brow-wall′i-a).

Although this genus is native to tropical America, it commemorates a Swedish bishop. It deserves attention for its rich blue flowers and its compact habit of growth. Because it re-

[ 24 ]

quires a longer time than most annuals to develop flowers, Browallia is, unfortunately, little known.

The species B. elata or B. demissa bears a profusion of miniature flowers which are either blue or violet. A white form is available also. This compact annual, averaging eighteen inches in height, may, after its summer bloom, be cut back and taken indoors for the window garden. Undoubtedly, B. speciosa major is the finest of all, with its large ultramarine-blue flowers often an inch or more across. While seldom seen in gardens, it proves satisfactory when grown in a sheltered spot; plant it in masses for landscape effect. B. viscosa compacta, Sapphire, is a compact form with intense dark blue flowers accentuated with a white eye. It makes a desirable border plant, since it seldom grows more than ten inches tall.

Start the seed in a greenhouse or in a sunny window and set the plants of B. viscosa six inches apart. B. speciosa major and B. elata require more space, since they average eighteen to twenty inches high. Grow the plants in full sun or partial shade, and give them rich soil.

## CACALIA (ka-kay'li-a). TASSEL FLOWER

The Tassel Flower, or Flora's Paintbrush, as it is sometimes called, should not be confused with the Devil's Paintbrush, Hieracium aurantiacum, one of our dangerous common weeds. The name Cacalia is of ancient Greek origin, and the more correct name, Emilia, seems to have no recognized significance, and is seldom used. Slender but sturdy stems, eighteen inches long, support the clusters of dainty orange-scarlet tassels of this tropical annual. These are followed by silky balloon-like heads of seed. While the Tassel Flower is not as showy as many annuals, it is useful for interplanting among low perennials like Primulas or other spring-blooming plants. As a cut-flower it lends a delicate touch of orange to flower arrangements. There is also a yellow form.

The seed may be sown outside, and successive sowings should be made if one would have a continuous display of flowers. Set the plants six inches apart in full sun or partial shade.

## CALENDULA (ka-len'dew-la). POT MARIGOLD

The Common or Pot Marigold of old English gardens is a plant steeped in tradition. Its botanical name Calendula hails from the Latin, meaning "first day of the month," in reference to its vigor in blooming. In Chaucer's time it was called Gold-flower. Also known as the "Sunne's Hearbe" and the "Sunne's Bride," it was the "Winking Mary-bud" in Shakespeare's play "Cymbeline." Valued as a pot-herb, it was used also as a remedy for sore teeth and as "a comforter of the heart and spirits." In nosegays arranged with hearts-ease or johnny-jump-ups it signified "happiness stored in recollections."

The greatly improved Calendulas we grow today are a far cry from the "Winking Mary-buds" of Elizabethan times. Not only have they been improved in size and in color, but pleasing quilled kinds are now grown.

Campfire (Sensation) is a brilliant orange with a scarlet sheen. The rich yellow chrysanthemum-like flowers of Chrysantha or Sunshine (illustrated on page 23) brought this strain recognition in the 1934 All-America Selections. Then there is Orange Fantasy, one of the 1938 All-America Selections, with large orange blooms accentuated by mahogany centers, and Orange Shaggy (also an All-America Selection), a loosely formed flower with irregularly arranged petals. Radio is distinguished for its deep yellow quilled petals. In addition, there are several strains and mixtures listed by most seedsmen which are worth growing. The wide variations found in packets of mixed seeds are always a pleasant surprise.

Few cultural directions are necessary since the seed germinates with ease in a greenhouse, in a coldframe, or in the open ground. Give the plants full sun, fertile soil, and keep the seed-pods pinched off. Allow twelve inches of space between plants.

## CALLIOPSIS (kal-e-op'sis). TICKSEED

Calliopsis, or more correctly Coreopsis, in its many forms is one of our most easily grown annuals. Some early botanist attached the Greek equivalent for "bug-like" to this genus because of the forms of the seed. Garden enthusiasts are not always aware of the value of commonplace annuals like Calliopsis until some hybridizer puts forth an improved form. Such is the case with Calliopsis, Golden Crest or Golden Crown (see illustration on page 24) which received an Award of Merit in the 1938 All-America Selections. It is an improved form of C. Drummondi, producing a fair percentage of semi-double blooms. The plants are compact in form and bear large golden yellow flowers on slender stems fifteen inches long. C. tinctoria produces clusters of flowers, with rich crimson-maroon and brown markings. The hybrid forms vary in height from nine inches to three feet.

Few annuals are easier to grow from seed, and few self-sow more readily—even to the point of becoming weeds. Plant Calliopsis in masses, scattering the seed broadcast. Varieties like Golden Crest should be set fifteen inches apart in full sun.

## CALLISTEPHUS (kal-lis′te-fus). CHINA ASTER

The botanical name of the China Aster means "beautiful crown," a most appropriate description for one of America's most popular annuals. (It is unfortunate that the colloquial name should include the word Aster, which signifies a widely distributed genus including many hardy native kinds.) Garden lovers owe much to Father d'Incarville, Jesuit Missionary to China, who introduced Callistephus to European gardens more than two hundred years ago. The original forms were single, and some enthusiasts still prefer single Asters to double hybrids.

Until a few years ago, there was hardly a garden where China Asters were not grown. But then several pests appeared on the scene, among them "Aster Wilt" and "Aster Yellows," both fungous diseases. In addition, there was the problem of root aphis, the tarnished plant bug, and the blister beetle. Aster Wilt has been overcome to a large extent by the development of wilt-resistant strains in nearly all the varieties in the trade. Aster Yellows can be checked only by growing Asters in cloth houses, a practice followed by many market gardeners, because the disease is carried by a leafhopper which can be excluded by this special treatment. In case either disease becomes evident in your garden, destroy at once all diseased plants by burning them. Root aphis may be controlled by using tobacco dust around the roots of the plants. The tarnished plant bug and the blister beetle do very considerable damage and spraying seems to restrain them but little. (Cloth houses will, of course, exclude them.) Grow only wilt-resistant Asters in your garden and keep them in active growth.

Despite the onslaught of insects and diseases, hybridizers have worked steadily to improve China Asters. Many distinct types are now listed. All are distinguished by their habit of growth, their flower structure, and their period of bloom. Few seedsmen sell all the varieties available, but practically every catalogue contains a representative list of the various types. No attempt has been made to mention the wide color-range which includes more than two hundred varieties. Turn to your favorite seed catalogue for individual colors, and select only those that are definitely stated to be wilt-resistant.

Giants of California are noted for their vigor of growth (two and one-half to three feet in height) and their large blooms with curled and interlaced petals. They are usually late in flowering, and include rose, pink, white, blue, and dark purple tones. Even larger, but more limited in coloring, are the extraordinary hybrids known as Super-Giants. Peony-flowered Asters are similar in height and season of bloom to the Giants of California, but the flowers vary in form. They are more compact, with shorter and broader petals, suggesting a more rounded and less shaggy appearance. Beauty Asters are classified here because they are similar in the structure of their petals, but the centers are incurved in such a way as to suggest a spiral; they flower in mid-season. American Beauty Asters are the late-flowering counterparts of the Beauty Asters.

Comet type Asters include the shaggy-petaled kinds of loose form and fluffy texture. Early Express or Early Wonder, a class of dwarf habit, averaging twelve to fifteen inches, is among the first to bloom. Astermum grows somewhat taller, fifteen to eighteen inches in height, coming into bloom several weeks after Early Express; these sturdy plants are effective garden material with flowers of varying sizes. Advancing in height and in season of bloom, the Giant Comets take their place; about two feet in height, they display their short-stemmed flowers in great profusion. Like all the old Aster types, the Ostrich Feather has had its plumes revamped and with stronger stems and larger flowers, the two-foot plants have taken on a new vigor, flowering in

CELOSIA PYRAMIDALIS, FLAME OF FIRE
*See page 33*

[ 29 ]

early fall. Here belong the Improved Crego varieties, noted for their vigorous branching habit. The two-and-one-half-foot plants send forth long-stemmed blooms in early September.

The flowers of the Branching types, in contrast to those of the Comet types, are more regular in outline, with broader petals more closely arranged, suggesting greater depth of form. According to season, first come the Early Dawn varieties, averaging fifteen inches in height. These are followed by the Improved

CENTAUREA, JUBILEE GEM
*See page 33*

Queen of the Market, which are usually eighteen inches or more in height. Next come the early Royal or Invincible Asters, slightly taller, and later in flowering. Giant Washington or Fall Upright Branching Asters usher in September; they are decidedly upright in their growth, varying from two to three feet. American Branching or Vick's Branching varieties have long been the glory of the September garden; the broad petals, which tend to whirl at the center, make sturdy blooms on long-stemmed plants which grow two and one-half feet or more. Heart of France, an unusual blood-red variety, belongs in this group.

The petals of King Asters are noticeably pointed and are best described as needle-like in appearance. Both branching and upright forms are grown; they bloom in midseason.

Aurora Asters have quilled centers, surrounded by several rows of flat petals. Outstanding in this class is the yellow Aster, Golden Sheaf, a tall-growing variety.

Pompon types are almost inevitable in a widely hybridized genus like the China Aster. Like Button Chrysanthemums, the flowers are small, rounded in form, and usually average a foot in height. The Imbricated Pompons have cushioned centers and Lilliput blooms that are flat in form, with quill-like petals.

As previously noted, the original Asters as introduced from China had single flowers. Fortunately, with the great amount of hybridizing that has been carried on, the beauty of the single type has not been lost. Several strains are offered by our leading seedsmen. The Single Giants of California grow two to three feet tall and produce their large blossoms on long stems in midseason. From English growers we have the Southcote Beauty Asters, with medium-sized blossoms on two-foot plants. Because they are more suggestive of single than double flowers, the California Sunshine Asters are included here. (See illustration on page 14.) Many gardeners prefer them to the double forms because of their striking petal formation. The innermost disc petals have a yellow glow, and these are surrounded by larger quilled petals, in addition to the slightly curved ray petals. Well-grown plants average two and one-half feet in height.

Disinfect the seed with Semesan or a formaldehyde solution before sowing. It may be started in a sunny window or in a coldframe. Space the tall branching kinds at least fifteen inches apart, and those of more dwarf habit accordingly. Rich sandy loam suits Asters best. Cultivate and water them freely during dry spells. Plants in vigorous growth are usually less susceptible to disease. Destroy all diseased plants.

## CAMPANULA (kam-pan'you-la). CANTERBURY BELL

Canterbury Bells bring to mind the immortal tales of old Geoffrey Chaucer and his Canterbury pilgrims. These old favorites are biennials, which need replacing every second year. However, there appeared among the 1933 All-America Selections an *annual* form of Canterbury Bells which produced flowers the first year from seed. While the flowers are not quite so large as the biennial varieties, the fact that they bloom the same season they are sown makes them desirable. Blue Bell is described as Cambridge blue; Mission Bell is a pink variety; Angelus Bell is rose, and the white form is Wedding Bell.

Since it takes six months to produce flowering plants, the seed should be started indoors in early February. Grow the plants in full sun, setting them nine to twelve inches apart. These Canterbury Bells enjoy rich soil.

CANDYTUFT. See Iberis, page 54.

## CELOSIA (sell-oh'si-a). COCKSCOMB

Botanical names often puzzle amateur gardeners, but the use of Greek and Latin makes them flexible internationally. Yet these scientific terms sometimes are baffling until one knows their meaning. The name Celosia is derived from the Greek, meaning "burned," in reference to the brilliant red blossoms. Even a fleeting glance at the crested or plumed varieties immediately convinces one of the flame-like form and color of these curiously interesting plants. They came to us originally from the tropics, and are commonly and appropriately known as Cockscombs.

Most familiar of all is the true Cockscomb, C. cristata, suggestive of the Victorian age of horse-hair and plush. Its strangely crested flowers are not unlike the combs of the barnyard fowl. These velvety-textured blossoms, varying in color from crimson to gold, are sometimes eight inches or more in length and are usually six to twelve inches tall. The plumed Cockscombs, C.

argentea or C. plumosa, are similar in color-range, but the flowers are pyramidal in form, tapering to a point like silky feathers. Well-grown plants sometimes reach three feet in height. The Chinese Woolflower, C. Childsi, is a garden hybrid having many characteristics of the plumed Cockscomb, save that its flowers form rounded heads. Another hybrid is C. pyramidalis, Flame of Fire, which won recognition in the 1934 All-America Selections. (See illustration on page 29.)

Sow the seed in a coldframe or in the open ground. Give the plants full sun and rich soil (if possible), since they respond readily to special feeding. Seedlings of C. cristata require nine to twelve inches between plants, and those of the tall-growing species need eighteen inches. Some gardeners grow all three kinds as pot-plants.

## CENTAUREA (sen-tor'ree-a). CORNFLOWER

It was the old Greek doctor Dioscorides who named this plant for the centaur Chiron, because it was believed to have cured an arrow wound in the centaur's foot. Few annuals are more popular than Centaurea cyanus, known also as Bachelor Button, Blue Bottle, and Cornflower. Strangely enough, one seldom sees our native American species, C. americana, or the fluffy Sweet Sultan, C. moschatus.

C. americana, the Basket-Flower, is found growing wild in the desert sands of Mexico and adjoining states. The plants often grow three feet tall or more, producing large, shaggy pink blossoms on stiff stems. A white form is also available. For background plantings they are most effective. Bachelor Buttons (C. cyanus) have so long been associated with American gardens that it is easy to understand how they have escaped from cultivation and become naturalized in western New York, Nebraska, Virginia, and parts of Canada. Once planted, Bachelor Buttons are a part of the garden, despite efforts to eradicate them. In addition to the rich blue shades, there are white, ruby-red, and rose forms of equal beauty. A variety called Jubilee Gem, recognized in the 1937 All-America Selections, is more compact than the type. (See the illustration on page 30.) C. moschatus or C. imperialis, better known as Sweet Sultan, has delightfully sweet-scented tassel-like flowers of silky texture on stems twelve to fifteen inches long. The varied color-range of white, pink, red, lilac, and yellow blossoms on slender stems is a boon to those interested in the art of flower arrangement.

Seed of C. americana may be started in a coldframe or in the open ground. Allow twelve to fifteen inches between the plants. For early bloom, Bachelor Buttons are best planted in the late fall; if flowers are desired for the midsummer garden, seed may be sown in the open ground. Set the plants nine inches apart. C. moschatus does not transplant easily; hence the seed is best sown in the open where the plants are to bloom. Eliminate weak plants and thin the seedlings to stand six to nine inches apart. For a continuous supply of blossoms, make several sowings.

CHINA ASTER. See Callistephus, page 27.

## CHRYSANTHEMUM, ANNUAL (kris-san'thee-mum).

To many gardeners, the name Chrysanthemum conveys a picture of the hardy autumn-blooming kinds and the large-flowered varieties in florists' shops. The name means "golden flower," and is appropriately associated with the annual kinds, especially since many of the varieties are yellow or have yellow coloring in their petals.

Those commonly known as Painted Daisies are hybrids of C. carinatum, from Morocco. Conspicuous for their dark centers, the tri-colored flowers are further accentuated by distinctive bands of red, yellow, or brown. The foliage is sparse and skeleton-like. C. coronarium, the Crown Daisy, is known for its bushy growth and its double and semi-double flowers, ranging from white to deep yellow. An outstanding hybrid of vigorous habit is the new Golden Crown. The Corn Marigold of English cornfields, C. segetum, grows two to three feet tall, with single flowers which vary in color, as do the hybrids of C. carinatum. For their wide color-range, their free-flowering habit, and their use as cut-flowers, annual Chrysanthemums are most desirable. For showy effects in the garden, plant them in masses.

Sow the seed outside, and set the plants at least a foot apart in full sun. Pinch back the young seedlings to produce bushy plants; keep the seed-pods picked off. It is hardly advisable to grow them in partial shade because they tend to grow spindly and topple over.

COSMOS, ORANGE FLARE
*See page 39*

UNWIN'S HYBRID DAHLIAS
See page 41

CLARKIA (clark′i-a). CLARKIA

One of our native plants with an historical American name,
Clarkia honors Captain Clark, who, with his companion, Lewis,
discovered it in the Rocky Mountains of the Northwest more

than a hundred years ago.  This pleasing annual is sometimes disappointing, especially during long rainy periods.  Many fine double hybrids of C. elegans have been developed, in a wide variety of colors from pure white to the most brilliant orange-scarlet.  While the hybrids of this species are sometimes two feet tall or more, those of C. pulchelia are more compact, with a maximum height of eighteen inches.

Clarkia grows easily from seed sown in the open ground.  Pinch back the small plants to make them bushy, and give them ample sunlight.

## CLEOME (klee-oh'me).  SPIDER FLOWER

Cleome, with its great heads of papilionaceous-like flowers, is one of the big-scale annuals which earn a favorite place in many gardens.  The common name, Spider Flower, presumably refers to the spider-like form of the flowers, but from a distance the flower-heads look like an assembly of butterflies.  Cleome

GOURDS IN VARIETY
*See page 51*
[ 37 ]

usually grows three to four feet tall and makes an effective display among shrubs or perennials. The rose-pink flower-heads are of no value for cutting but continue to open fresh flowers over a long season.

Sow the seed in a coldframe or in the open ground. To grow specimens, set the plants eighteen inches apart. Among shrubs, plant them closer together, in groups of five or more. They thrive best in hot, dry areas, but will grow in partial shade.

CONVOLVULUS. See Ipomœa, page 55.

## COSMOS (kos'mus). Cosmos

What would a garden be without Cosmos? The derivation of the Greek name means "ornament," appropriately signifying the use of this annual in the garden and in the home. Whether planted in rows, or for background effects with other annuals, or as color masses in the perennial planting or shrub border, Cosmos dominates the scene.

Few plants require so little care or self-sow so readily as Cosmos. Crimson, pink, and white varieties are found in both early- and late-flowering kinds, which vary in height from two and one-half to five feet or more. The double-crested forms are among the hybrids of recent years, and the orange-yellow varieties have widened considerably the color-range of this indispensable annual. Among the early types are the Early Express and the Sensation strain. Both are obtainable in crimson, pink, and white; the Sensation strain is the taller, with immense blooms. The late-flowering kinds often grow five feet or more in height and do not bloom until September; accordingly, in regions where frosts come early, it is wise to grow the early-blooming types. This is true also of the double-crested or anemone-flowered kinds. Although not as tall or free-flowering as the single varieties, they are well worth growing, especially as cut-flowers. Two yellow-flowering varieties are outstanding: Klondyke, a late bloomer, and Klondyke, Orange Flare (Gold Medal, 1935 All-America Selections), which flowers in nine to twelve weeks from seed. (See illustration on page 35.)

Sow the seed in a coldframe or in the open ground, and set the plants

HEAVENLY BLUE MORNING-GLORIES
*See page 57*

eighteen to twenty-four inches apart. Cosmos thrive in almost any kind of soil. They tolerate partial shade, but grow best in full sun. If the seedlings become spindly, pinch them back or transplant them several times.

## CUPHEA (kew'fee-a). CUPHEA

The name Cuphea usually brings to mind the curious Cigar-Plant, C. ignea or C. platycentra, often used as a bedding plant. This Mexican genus takes its name from the Greek, meaning "curved," in reference to the structure of the flowers of some species. From Bodger's great California seed ranches, a novelty sort known as Firefly was introduced (season 1937-38) to American gardens. One glance at the delicately cut cerise-red flowers convinces the observer of the appropriateness of the name Firefly. The showy blooms and the compact habit of the plant, averaging ten inches in height, make it ideal for edging.

The Cuphea is a tender annual which may be started in a sunny window or a coldframe, since it takes twelve to fourteen weeks to produce flowering plants. Set the plants four to six inches apart, in full sun.

## CYNOGLOSSUM (sin-o-gloss'um). HOUNDS-TONGUE

Probably best described as a tall forget-me-not, the species Cynoglossum amabile, by nature a biennial, is often found in annual gardens. This native of eastern Asia is also called the Chinese Forget-me-not; Hounds-Tongue, the English equivalent of the Greek name, refers to the shape and rough character of the leaves. For a dominant note of blue in the garden, it needs to be planted in masses. Well-grown plants are often eighteen to twenty-four inches tall, thus providing ideal material for flower arrangements. A pink variety is also available.

Since this plant is by nature a biennial, the seed needs to be started early in a greenhouse or coldframe. Frequently, plants started in the open ground fail to bloom, and they seldom live over winter satisfactorily. Transfer the seedlings to flats or individual pots before setting them in the open ground, since they do not transplant easily. Allow six to nine inches between plants.

## DAHLIA (dahl'ya). DAHLIA

For many gardeners who have neither the space nor the enthusiasm for large exhibition types of Dahlias, there are several dwarf-growing kinds with small flowers which bloom the first year from seed. Although classified as tender perennials, desirable strains with both single and double flowers are obtainable from seed, and are usually grown as annuals. Named for a Swedish botanist, Dahlias were first collected in Mexico about 1570 by Francisco Hernandez, physician to Philip II of Spain.

Dwarf bedding Dahlias lend themselves to many uses in the garden. They provide a continuous display of color for the shrub border and the perennial planting, as well as for the annual garden. In small gardens, it may be possible to grow only a few plants, but these few will supply many good cut-flowers for indoor arrangements. Several strains of hybrids are offered by seedsmen. The Coltness Hybrids grow eighteen to twenty-four inches tall, bearing single flowers in several shades, including red, orange, yellow, and pink. Unique shapes are found in the orchid-flowered kinds which are sometimes listed as Starfish, because of the crimped and twisted petals which give the appearance of stars. Mignon Dahlias represent a free-flowering strain, and Unwin's Hybrids (see illustration, page 36) are distinguished for their semi-double flowers.

Raising Dahlias from seed offers few difficulties. It is best sown indoors in early March, and the young plants may be set at least eighteen inches apart in full sun. Since late frosts are detrimental to the young growth, care must be taken not to transfer the plants to the open ground until the soil is warm. Pinch the centers to produce branching plants. Favorite colors may be carried over winter by storing the tuberous roots.

## D A T U R A (dah-teu′ra). TRUMPET-FLOWER

From far-away India came this harmless relative of the poisonous Jimson-weed. Scholars tell us that its name is derived from the Arabic, and botanists remind us that it belongs to the potato family.

These giant cone-shaped flowers, large enough to provide a trumpet for Gabriel, are familiarly known as Angel's-Trumpet or Trumpet-Flower. Datura cornucopia (D. fastuosa) is one of those big-scale annuals which deserve a place in the shrub border or the large annual garden. The rather coarse tropical foliage is of little consequence in comparison with the huge trumpets, sometimes eight inches long. Purplish tones mark the outer surface, in contrast to the white inner portion from which is emitted a sweet fragrance.

If one would fully enjoy this tropical annual, the seed needs to be started indoors or in a coldframe in late March or early April. Since well-developed plants grow three feet or more in height, and spread an equal distance, set them eighteen to twenty-four inches apart. Grow them in rich loam.

## DELPHINIUM (dell-fin′i-um). LARKSPUR

Outstanding among the tall-growing annuals are the many hybrids of Delphinium Consolida and D. Ajacis, which are easily distinguished from the perennial species by their foliage and flowers. The name Delphinium, from the Greek, meaning "dolphin," is associated with the shape of the individual blooms. With their quaint, spire-like forms, which sometimes suggest antique candelabra, these excellent and easy annuals are well adapted as accent plants for large mass effects, and for middle-ground or background groups in borders. Some gardeners prefer to grow them in combination with other annuals, while others allow them to self-grow yearly in the perennial border.

The Giant Imperial Strain (see Frontispiece illustration) produces three-foot spikes of flowers in many tints and shades. Among them are: Blue Spire; Carmine King; Coral King; Exquisite, a rich pink; Gloria, deep rose; La France, salmon-pink; Lilac Spire; Sweet Lavender; and White Spire. Perhaps the most vivid of the dwarf Larkspurs is the delightful D. grandiflorum (D. chinense or sinense) which is seldom more than two feet tall. Although a perennial, it is often grown as an annual, since the seed germinates readily. The loosely arranged panicles of brilliant blue are highly treasured for cutting.

Since annual Larkspurs do not transplant easily and are truly hardy, it is best to sow the seed where they are to flower. This may be done in early spring or in the fall, particularly if one desires an early crop of flowers. To hasten the germination of the seed, wrap it in a cloth and subject it to alternate thawing and freezing for several days. Mix a little sand with the seed for more even distribution, and thin the plants to stand at least nine inches apart. A sunny location or light shade suits them, and they prefer rich loam to stony soil because of their slender tap-roots. Start the seed of D. grandiflorum indoors or in a coldframe, and, as this species endures

CHRYSANTHEMUM-FLOWERED AFRICAN MARIGOLDS
*See page 82*

transplanting, set the plants nine inches apart. If the soil is inclined to be strongly acid, dig in a little agricultural lime.

## DIANTHUS (dy-an'thus). PINKS

We call them Pinks or Carnations, but the Elizabethans knew them as Gillyflowers and Sops in Wine. The old Greek name Dianthus, meaning "divine flower," may have been attached to them because of their delightful fragrance. In the sixteenth century, Dianthus fragrance was a source of great interest, as recorded in the writings of Thomas Hyll. He told of several fantastic methods by which the cinnamon or clove

African Marigold, Yellow Supreme
*See page 82*

[ 44 ]

fragrance could be increased in the flower. Today many species of Dianthus in addition to Carnations (D. caryophyllus) are grown in gardens. We have turned our attention especially to kinds for borders and rock-gardens, among them many annual varieties.

Carnations in the garden are not always satisfactory, particularly in areas where the summers are extremely warm or very moist. They prefer a cool, somewhat moist atmosphere. In rich loam they produce satisfactory results, even when planted in partial shade. When adequate staking is not possible, it is best to cut the blooms as soon as they open in order to enjoy them indoors, because the stems are easily broken by rain and wind. Chabaud's strain is most suitable for the average garden, but it is hardly advisable for beginners to grow Carnations.

On the whole, the hybrids of D. chinensis, the China Pinks, are much more satisfactory in the average garden than are the true Carnations. They usually grow twelve to fifteen inches high, and may be used for edging, bedding, and rock-garden plantings. Many varieties bearing single, double, and fringed flowers are grown, usually in mixed colors. The forms of Diadematus, with flowers in the lilac, purple, and crimson range; Heddewigi, with its chintz-like combinations of color; and Laciniatus, with its fringed petals, are all worth growing.

Gardeners should not overlook D. hybridus, Sweet Wivelsfield, which was developed from D. Allwoodi and D. barbatus (Sweet William). The free-flowering plants are compact in habit, growing ten to twelve inches high. Where the winters are mild, the plant is a true biennial.

Annual Carnation seed and Sweet Wivelsfield may be started in a sunny window during February, or in a coldframe in early March. Set the plants nine inches apart in rich soil. China Pinks are easily grown from seed sown in a coldframe or in the open. The plants need to be set six inches apart, in full sun, and, if possible, in rich soil. Feed the plants occasionally with liquid manure and remove all weak growth and seed-pods to keep the plants in good blooming condition.

## DIDISCUS (di-dis'kus). BLUE LACE-FLOWER

Garden books of fifty years ago recognized this Australian plant as Trachymene cærulea, but the old name Didiscus still persists. This miniature edition, in soft lavender-blue, of one of the most admired and cursed of our native plants, Queen Anne's Lace, is most appropriately known as Blue Lace-Flower. It is hardly pronounced enough in color to make a display in the garden, but it is one of the most decorative of cut-flowers.

The plants grow best in full sun and vary in height from twelve to eighteen inches, according to the fertility of the soil. Sow the seed indoors, in a coldframe, or in the open ground, and set the seedlings nine inches apart. Pinch the plants to make them branch, and, if possible, grow them in rich soil. Applications of liquid manure are helpful.

## DIMORPHOTHECA (dy-more-fo-thee'ka). CAPE-MARI-GOLD

A hasty glance at this bothersome name gives little suggestion of the beauty of these gaily colored daisies from South Africa. It is one of those Greek names referring to the form of the clustered florets in the center of the flower. Essentially an annual for the warm, sunny parts of the garden, Dimorphotheca is desirable for massed effects in borders, as a foreground planting for shrubs or perennials, or with other annuals. The showy flowers are borne on wiry stems a little more than a foot high. Dimorphotheca aurantiaca is brilliant orange with a dark center, and there are varieties bearing salmon and yellow flowers. The species D. annua ringens, of more dwarf habit, has grayish flowers with blue zonal markings.

Sow the seed where the plants are to grow, and thin to allow six to nine inches between them. Since they bloom freely and tend to exhaust themselves, it may be necessary to make two sowings for a succession of flowers.

## ESCHSCHOLTZIA (esh-sholt'zi-a). CALIFORNIA POPPY

If we could Americanize this tongue-twisting name (commemorating a German botanist) by eliminating one "sch," the botanical name of the dainty California Poppy would be less perplexing. Exquisite in form and color, these objects of fleeting beauty are further enhanced by the finely cut foliage which lends a note of blue-green to complete a pleasing contrast of nature.

Annuals for the hottest part of the garden, California Poppies need ample space in which to display themselves to best advantage. They make bushy plants, twelve to fifteen inches tall, and are sometimes interplanted with narcissi and tulips to carry on a succession of bloom. When seed is sown before the tulip buds open, the seedlings make a pleasing mass of green which helps to conceal the decaying bulb foliage. Eschscholtzia aurantiaca (Orange King), E. californica, and Golden West are outstanding varieties. Mauve Beauty, a lavender-mauve; the Ramona hybrids, with ruffled petals; The Geisha, golden yellow, suffused with crimson; and Vesuvius, coppery red, are more erect than the type. Semi-double kinds are sometimes grown.

Sow the seed where the plants are to bloom and thin to stand nine inches apart. Like most Poppies, they are not transplanted easily; hence it is best to mix the tiny seeds with sand and scatter them broadcast.

## EUPHORBIA (you-for'bi-a). SNOW-ON-THE-MOUNTAIN

There is hardly a gardener who does not know Snow-on-the-Mountain. Few plants have been more appropriately named than this wide-spread American species, Euphorbia marginata, which grows wild in many places from Minnesota to Texas. The botanical name, which was used by Pliny nearly two thousand years ago, is said to commemorate an ancient king. Snow-on-the-Mountain combines well with other annuals and perennials, serving as a garden highlight. A showy cut-flower, it is often used as a filler with large flowers for decorative effects.

Truly a "hard-luck" plant, it is not particular as to soil, and will grow in partial shade as well as in sunny areas. Furthermore, it self-sows readily. In hot, dry places the plant grows compactly and does not require staking.

FOUR-O'CLOCK. See Mirabilis, page 63.

## GAILLARDIA (gay-lar'di-a). BLANKET-FLOWER

For their brilliance of color, their vigor of growth, and their value as cut-flowers, few plants surpass the annual Gaillardias. Although native to the warm, dry regions of our own country, this genus took its name from a French patron of botany. The gaily colored blossoms are well named Blanket-Flowers, because they often rival the brilliant colorings of Indian blankets. The perennial form, Gaillardia aristata, is very similar.

Gaillardia pulchella is the source of many of our hybrids, which range from the rich red of Indian Chief to the yellowish or white blossom of The Bride, and include many showy combinations in a wide variety of colors.

The seed may be sown directly in the open ground, and the plants need at least a square foot of space in which to develop. Plant them in full sun, keep the seed-pods from developing, and Gaillardias will bloom persistently.

## GAZANIA (ga-zay'ni-a). GAZANIA

This plant-name brings to mind Theodore Gaza, who translated into Latin the botanical writings of the Greek doctor Theophrastus, in the fifteenth century. From South Africa came this dwarf annual with its daisy-like flowers. Hybrids of G. splendens, developed in recent years by Bodger in California, where it is used in street planting and is treated as a half-hardy perennial, produce delightful daisy-like flowers of orange and yellow of varying intensity.

Sow the seed in a coldframe or in the open ground, and give the plants a hot, dry situation in the garden. Sandy soil suits them well, and they seldom grow more than ten inches high, making a somewhat procumbent mass of foliage and flowers.

## GILIA (gil'li-a). GILIA

Some annuals are continually overlooked by amateur gardeners for no accountable reason. Among them are several species of the genus Gilia, which is native in the Lower South and along the West Coast.

Gilia capitata, with its abundant heads of soft blue blossoms on eighteen-inch stems among dainty foliage, is a delightful cut-flower. The individual plants are of free-branching habit. Comparatively little known are the gay coral spires of the Texas-Plume, G. coronopifolia or rubra. Although this plant is usually classed as a biennial, it may be treated as annual if the seed is sown early enough, and that attention is well repaid, for this little-appreciated native plant produces showy flower-spikes two and one-half to three feet tall. These are highly decorative as cut-flowers or as accent plants in the garden. As its name

FRENCH MARIGOLD, HARMONY
*See page 84*

suggests, G. tricolor, the Birds-Eye Gilia, is a combination of three hues; the blooms range from violet to rose with rich purple throats, in contrast to the yellow tubes. Eighteen inches seems to be its limit, and it makes a compact mass.

G. capitata and G. tricolor may be treated as half-hardy annuals. Sow the seed in a coldframe for early bloom, or in the open ground. Set the plants nine inches apart in a sunny location. Their soil-requirements are ordinary. To grow G. coronopifolia successfully, start the seed indoors in February, since it requires a longer time to produce blooming plants. Allow twelve to fifteen inches between plants, and give them rich soil and a sunny location.

## GODETIA (go-dee'she-a). GODETIA

Like Gilia, this genus is native to the West Coast, but it is unlike it in adaptability. It takes its name from a Swiss botanist.

GLORIOUS GLEAM HYBRID NASTURTIUMS
*See page 89*

Godetia thrives best in a cool climate, and does well in partial
shade. English gardeners grow it to perfection, and as a result,
many delightful hybrids are in cultivation. Several azalea-
flowered hybrids with double flowers of satiny texture and great
depth of color, dominantly in the red sector, are available from
American growers. Success with Godetias is a guerdon of garden
capability.

For early bloom, start the seed in a coldframe in late March or early

April, and set the plants out in a partially shaded area; or put the seed in the open ground. Place Godetia in masses, with the plants nine inches apart.

## GOMPHRENA (gom-free'na). GLOBE AMARANTH

Everlastings have a peculiar fascination for many amateur gardeners, and particularly for beginners. Perhaps it is the papery texture of the flowers, or it may be the long-lasting qualities which these Strawflowers possess. At any rate, they are curious and interesting, and well worth growing. Gomphrena, or Globe Amaranth, inherits its name from the days of Pliny. It is sometimes referred to as Bachelor Button. The plants grow twelve to fifteen inches tall, are of compact form and free-flowering habit. Shades of rose, purple, and white seem to predominate in these globular flowers.

The seed may be sown in the open ground. Grow the plants in masses, and space them at least six inches apart. Full sun suits them best; they have no particular soil-preference.

## GOURDS

From the standpoint of utility, Gourds have been cultivated for many generations, but in recent years their decorative value has been appreciated (see illustration, page 37). The name Gourd is generally applied to those durable fruits valued for decoration and use. However, the family Cucurbitaceæ includes melons, pumpkins, and squashes. Growing Gourds offers many surprises because of the unique forms of the fruits and flowers. Beginners usually buy seed in mixed packets, but collectors aim to grow the many species of several genera. These trailing plants scramble easily over old fences or along the ground. Some gardeners grow them on wire fences. For many years Gourds have fascinated Dr. L. H. Bailey. His book, "The Garden of Gourds," records the interesting story of this unusual family.

Plant the seed in hills four to six feet apart, like squash or melons. Use several seeds in each hill. Gourds thrive best in a warm, sunny location, and the seed should not be planted until all danger of frost is past. Do not harvest the fruits until they are ripe and the colors are fully developed. Set them in a warm, dry place and remove all soil from the hard shells. Some gardeners polish them with floor wax and others shellac the surfaces. Those not satisfied with the natural colors paint them.

## GYPSOPHILA (jip-sof'fill-a). BABYS-BREATH

Annual Babys-Breath is, perhaps, best suited to the cutting garden, although it is sometimes used for interplanting with tall-growing annuals and summer-flowering bulbs. From its Greek specific name one learns that it is a lime-loving plant. This annual is of sufficient value to warrant several sowings each year, especially since it blooms six weeks after sowing, thus completing its cycle of growth in a comparatively short time. Several improved forms are now available. Among them are Gypsophila elegans grandiflora, the large-flowering kind; a pink variety, G. elegans rosea; and G. muralis, a dwarf, procumbent variety with pink flowers, which is suitable for the rock-garden.

When growing the plants for cut-flowers, buy the seed by the ounce, sow it in rows, and thin the plants to stand at least six to nine inches apart in a sunny location. For a continuous supply of blooms make sowings at intervals of two weeks. It frequently self-sows, producing vigorous plants.

## HELIANTHUS (he-li-an'thus). SUNFLOWER

While the huge Sunflowers which the painter Van Gogh has made so famous are not desirable or adaptable to many small gardens, there are the delightful "cut-and-come-again" varieties. Yet there are some gardeners who find it imperative to grow the large Sunflowers for feeding birds, or because these upstanding old sentinels belong in certain locations. In the ancient Inca civilization, the Sunflower was a sacred symbol of the sun-worshiping natives, and in Russia the seeds are eaten like peanuts. The old Greek name means Sun Flower.

Those giant plants which often grow to eight feet or more in height, with their large open centers, are for only a few gardens. Then there are several less obtrusive double forms, and a red-flowering kind. For small gardens, there are the hybrids of Helianthus cucumerifolius which average four feet in height. Some have flowers with twisted petals, and some are very dwarf in habit.

Sow the seed in the open ground; give the plants a sunny location with at least two feet of space each way. Then watch them grow. Pinch back the dwarf-growing kinds to produce bushy plants.

## HELICHRYSUM (hell-i-kry'zum). STRAWFLOWER

The most familiar of all the Everlastings or Strawflowers is the genus Helichrysum. This name, derived from the Greek, means "sun gold," a reference to the rich yellow centers of the papery flowers. Sturdy in its growth, often reaching two and one-half feet or more in height, this Australian annual readily provides a colorful mass when planted in beds or with other annuals. Red, rose-pink, yellow, violet, and white varieties are obtainable in separate colors. Recently a strain of dwarf hybrids, averaging about fifteen inches in height, has been introduced.

Plant the seed in a coldframe or in the open ground. Set the seedlings fifteen inches apart, in a sunny location. (When growing Helichrysums in quantity, the plants are usually set in rows.) For winter bouquets, cut the flowers *before* they have expanded fully, remove the foliage, and hang the blooms in a dark place, with their heads down, until dry. Even the tiny buds will expand, and they are more attractive than the larger flowers.

## HUNNEMANNIA (hun-nee-man'i-a). GOLDEN-CUP

Like Argemone and Eschscholtzia, the genus Hunnemannia is a member of the widely cultivated Poppy family, but is not extensively grown. Its five-syllable name commemorates an English botanist. Some gardeners prefer to call it Giant Yellow Tulip-Poppy, Golden-Cup, or Mexican Tulip-Poppy because it is indigenous to the hot, dry regions of Mexico. The flowers somewhat resemble those of the California Poppy, but are larger and more cup-like. Hunnemannia fumariæfolia, with its single yellow chalices on eighteen-inch stems among the attractive bluish green foliage, and the hybrid Sunlite, a 1934 All-America Selection having so-called semi-double flowers, are listed by most seedsmen. The blooms close toward evening, but the variety Sunlite has the advantage of colored bracts which remain open, giving the flower a unique form.

Full sun and dry soil offer no difficulties for this sturdy annual. Plant it near some blue-flowering annual like Gilia capitata. Because of its true Poppy-like nature, it is not transplanted easily. Mix the seed with sand and sow it in the open ground. Thin out to allow nine inches between seedlings. If it becomes necessary to transplant, lift each seedling, preferably the smaller ones, with a ball of moist earth.

[ 53 ]

## IBERIS (eye-beer'is). CANDYTUFT

Candytuft is one of the old-fashioned hardy annuals expressing much of the charm of Victorian gardens, possibly because of the prim arrangement of its flat flower-heads. Iberis is derived from Iberia, the ancient name of Spain, where several species grow naturally.

In many gardens, midsummer cutting material would be scarce were it not for such rapid-growing annuals as Candytuft. Because its blooming season is comparatively short, it cannot be planted in large masses, as one would Petunias, Zinnias, or Marigolds. Rather, it belongs in the cutting garden or in a part of the garden where it can be replaced with other plants. The two annual species, Iberis amara, the Rocket Candytuft, and I. umbellata, the Globe Candytuft, have produced the hybrid strains commonly grown. The Rocket form is distinguished for its white columnar flower-spikes on fifteen-inch stems, known as Empress or Hyacinth-flowered types; whereas the Globe form, on slightly shorter stems, has flat flower-heads of varying shades of carmine, rose, lavender, and purple. Compact varieties of both kinds are obtainable.

Sow seed outdoors and thin the plants to stand six inches apart. It grows well in full sun or partial shade and self-sows readily. Liquid manure improves the large-flowering kinds, but this annual requires no coddling.

## IMPATIENS (im-pay'she-enz). BALSAM

A subtropical plant often seen in old gardens, the sturdy Balsam suggests Victorian primness with its short, bushy growth, its brightly colored double flowers borne close to the stems, and the curious whorl-like arrangement of the leaves. Indeed, its whole aspect is decidedly quaint. It seems to have become an established favorite with the Polish peasants, who often grow it as a pot-plant. The name Touch-me-not, often applied to it, refers to the ripe seed-pods which snap open when touched, scattering the seed broadcast. The Latin name has the same significance.

Care must be taken not to plant the seed until the soil is warm. If transplanted several times and spaced twelve to fifteen inches apart each way, the seedlings will develop vigorous plants.

NICOTIANA, SNOWSTORM
*See page 67*

IPOMŒA (ip-po-mee'a or eye-poh-mee'ah). MORNING-GLORY

Morning-Glories have long been popular garden plants, but the introduction of the variety Heavenly Blue placed the genus in the upper bracket of desirable annuals. The old Greek name

[ 55 ]

GIANT-FLOWERING PANSIES
*See page 93*

Ipomœa means "like bindweed," a reference to the twining stems. Many species in this genus have been listed as Convolvulus, the botanical name for bindweed.

In recent years, few flowers have had greater appeal alike for the garden enthusiast and the casual observer. There is something indescribably beautiful about those great blue trumpets, borne in great profusion and usually perched high on trellises or arbors. In dull weather, they remain open nearly all day, but the hot sun of midsummer quickly wilts the delicate blooms. Yet they are the joy of the morning garden and hold up well until the sun is high in the heavens. It is important to obtain seed of the Early or Improved Heavenly Blue (see illustration, page 38) because it flowers earlier than the original hybrid. Giant Pink is another popular variety color.

Comparatively little known are the semi-double and double rose-pink flowers of Rose Marie. The Moonflower, listed as Ipomœa mexicana alba, bears its large white blooms at night.

In Japan, Morning-Glories are widely grown in pots, and many unusual strains are cultivated. These are usually listed as I. imperialis. The Brazilian Morning-Glory, I. setosa, is a rank grower, providing more shade than others, and bears large lavender-pink blooms often five inches across.

Morning-Glory seed does not always germinate easily. Some gardeners soak the seed over night or longer in warm water to soften the hard shell. Others nick one end of each seed with a knife or file and place the seed on moist sand, covering it with wet burlap until germination occurs. When this method is used, transplant the tiny seedlings into small pots, and set the plants out when the ground becomes warm. The seed may be sown indoors, in a coldframe, or where the plants are to bloom. Full sun or partial shade is satisfactory, but it is not necessary to have rich soil. In fact, that usually causes the growth of foliage rather than flowers.

## KOCHIA (ko'ke-a). Burning-Bush

Burning-Bush, Summer-Cypress, and Mexican Firebush are popular names for this easy annual, which at one stage resembles a small evergreen. This plant, named for a German botanist, has been used more frequently than many more desirable annuals. Yet it has a place in many gardens as an accent plant, and may sometimes be used as a dwarf hedge. While no one can object to the rich green texture of its foliage in summer, there is a difference of opinion about its autumn coloring, sometimes a purplish red. The plants average two and one-half feet in height.

Start the seed indoors or in the open ground and give the plants full sun; space them at least eighteen inches apart.

LARKSPUR. See Delphinium, page 42.

## LATHYRUS (lah'thi-russ). SWEET PEA

The old Greek name Lathyrus seems to have no recognized significance in connection with our modern Sweet Peas. Although introduced into England from Italy about 1700, it was not until the middle of the nineteenth century that gardeners gave them any serious attention. Since that time several thousand varieties have been introduced, and Sweet Peas are now among the most important cut-flowers in our florist shops and markets; the seedsmen grow tons of seed.

Sweet Peas are not equally successful in all parts of the United States. They need a cool temperature, and tend to weaken and wither in extreme heat. In many parts of New England and in the Northwest they grow successfully through the summer months. In the warmer sections of the country they are best grown as a spring crop. Since Sweet Peas are grown primarily as cut-flowers and have little decorative value in the garden, they are best grown in rows in the vegetable plot, or where they will not detract from the appearance of a well-planned garden.

Most seedsmen list summer- and winter-flowering kinds. The winter-flowering sorts, while especially adapted for forcing, are often grown in gardens because they bloom several weeks earlier than the summer-flowering types and thus prolong the blooming season. Blue, lavender, cerise, crimson, purple, salmon, orange, white, and many variations of pink are found among the named varieties. To list them would be to mention several hundred kinds. The variety Shirley Temple, illustrated on page 83, has a strong popular appeal for its color and its name.

Sweet Peas require more effort to obtain good results than do most annuals, but that effort is well repaid in the results that follow extra care. (Enthusiastic gardeners are not usually overwhelmed by the problem of hard work!) If possible, dig your trench in the fall, spading it to a depth of one and one-half to two feet and a foot in width. (Some gardeners have satisfactory results with trenches twelve inches deep.) Fill in with manure to a depth of several inches; then fill the trench with rich loam. Sweet Peas thrive best in fertile soil that is moist but well drained. Sow the seed as early as possible in the spring, covering to a depth of two inches, and thin the seedlings to stand six inches apart. To soften the hard seed-shell, the seed may be soaked in water over night. There are several other methods of starting the seed. It may be sown in the late fall before the ground freezes.

Cover the seed with soil to a depth of two inches and mulch the seed-bed well after the ground has frozen hard. (In the South seed is sown from November to February.) Many gardeners start their seed indoors in flats during February or early March, then transplant the seedlings to pots, and place in a coldframe until it is warm enough to set the plants in their permanent places. When the seedlings have reached six inches in height, they need supports. Brushwood or chicken wire may be used. Occasional applications of liquid manure, ample amounts of water, and frequent picking of the blooms are important factors in maintaining vigorous plants and a long blooming period.

## LAVATERA (la-va-tee′ra). TREE MALLOW

The Annual or Tree Mallow has never received the attention it deserves from amateurs, and yet it may well be called the counterpart of the large-flowering Hibiscus often found in perennial gardens. Named in honor of two Swiss plantsmen, the Lavater brothers of Linnæus' generation, this plant hails from the warm Mediterranean region.

Masses of this sturdy, tall-growing annual (usually three to four feet high and suggesting the name Tree Mallow) are most desirable for background effects in the annual garden, or for color splashes in the perennial border. The warm rose blossoms, hollyhock-like in appearance, and the rounded dull green leaves, are useful for arranging with other flowers.

Start the seed outside where the plants are to grow. The seedlings do not transplant readily because of their tap-roots, so characteristic of the Mallow family. It is not impossible to transplant them; some gardeners start them indoors and pot them before setting them out. Full sun suits Lavatera best.

## LINARIA (ly-nay′re-a). TOADFLAX

Toadflax is one of those annuals which might well be called a Dresden miniature among flowers. Its dainty blossoms, delicate in color and supported on slender stems, are often used in miniature flower arrangements, looking like tiny snapdragons. From far-away Morocco has come Linaria maroccana, which seldom grows more than ten inches high. Several shades of pink, yellow, violet, and white are available. An outstanding strain, recently introduced (Gold Medal, All-America Selections,

1934) is the Fairy Bouquet mixture, of compact habit and pleasing color-range. Grow Linaria in masses in the rock-garden, and save a place for this gem in the cutting garden.

Give it full sun. Sow seed in the open ground or in a coldframe and allow four to six inches between plants. Make several sowings for a succession of bloom. Often it self-sows, so that plants may appear the following year.

## LINUM (ly'num). FLAX

While the Flax of commerce, Linum usitatissimum, which provides us with linen and linseed oil, has no garden value, the Scarlet Flax, L. grandiflorum, from North Africa, brings an important note of scarlet to the summer garden. The plants average fifteen inches in height and are studded with brilliant red blossoms which in form are not unlike those of the hardy Blue Flax, L. perenne. To be sure, you would not plant Scarlet Flax near a bed of pink Petunias, but there are many places in the garden where it may be used to advantage.

Plant it in full sun, preferably in masses. The plants usually grow twelve inches tall and need to be four to six inches apart. For massed effects, mix the seed with sand and scatter it broadcast over the area.

## LOBELIA (lo-bee'le-a). LOBELIA

Many of our familiar garden plants are curiously international in their associations. The annual Lobelia, which sends forth myriads of miniature blue flowers in midsummer, came to us originally from South Africa. Strangely enough, it commemorates an early Flemish botanist, and is related to the brilliant cardinal flower which is native in wet places. Of the annual forms, Cambridge Blue is noted for its brilliance, and Crystal Palace for its deep blue flowers and rich dark foliage. Lobelia is ideally suited for edging beds and borders, and the trailing kind fits well into window- and porch-boxes.

The seed is usually planted indoors or in a coldframe in February or early March. It is hardly advisable to sow the seed in the open ground unless one lives in an area where the season is long. Many florists and small growers raise Lobelia in quantities, using cuttings of a selected strain, and it is usually easier to obtain plants than to grow them from seed.

## LUPINUS (loo-pine'us). LUPINE

Strangely enough, this exacting annual derives its name from the Latin meaning "wolf," an allusion to its supposed tendency to absorb soil-fertility. And yet, these spires of showy pea-like blossoms are much treasured by amateur gardeners, who often encounter many difficulties in attempting to grow them. Soil conditions undoubtedly constitute the major problem. Lupines belong to the great Legume family, which require an abundance of nitrogen for satisfactory growth. In many areas, where sufficient nitrogen is not available in the soil, it can be developed by adding the proper bacteria to the soil in the form of legume culture, obtainable from most seedsmen. Well-developed plants grow two feet tall. White, blue, purple, and pink varieties of Lupinus Hartwegi are available.

The Annual Lupines grow readily from seed, often flowering eight to ten weeks after sowing. The seed is best planted in the open ground where plants are to flower, since they do not transplant easily. Either full sun or partial shade suits them.

## LYCHNIS (lick'nis). CAMPION

Sometimes it seems as if the perplexities of life were almost as confusing as those of horticultural nomenclature. This genus now includes plants we used to know as Agrostemma and Viscaria, names which are still used in many catalogues. The genus name, meaning "lamp," reminds us of the brilliant red perennial species like Lychnis chalcedonica, Maltese Cross, and L. Haageana. Little appreciated in American gardens is L. Cœli-rosa, Rose-of-Heaven, also known as Agrostemma Cœli-rosa and Viscaria oculata. Like Lobelia, it makes a delightful edging plant. A rich rose shade and two shades of blue are offered.

Sow the seed in a coldframe or in the open ground. Set the plants in full sun, about six inches apart. They average ten to twelve inches in height.

MARIGOLD. See Tagetes, page 81.

## MATHIOLA (ma-thy'o-la). STOCK

In the days before scientific nomenclature had any great significance for amateur gardeners, carnations were known as

Gillyflowers, but after Shakespeare's time the name seems to have been transferred to Stocks (and less commonly to Wallflowers). This plant, native to southern Europe, is by nature a biennial but is best grown as an annual. It was named for an old Italian botanist, Matthiola.

For garden use it is important to select the early-blooming varieties, which should not be confused with those grown by florists for winter culture. The Ten-Weeks Stock comes into flower quickly (in approximately ten weeks, as the name implies) and averages fifteen inches in height. Lavender, purple, pink, white, soft yellow, and dark red are representative of the colors offered. A strain known as Cut-and-Come-Again is valued for its quantities of recurrent bloom because of the vigorous branching character of the two-foot plants. There are named varieties like Princess Alice, white; La France, rose; Brilliant, dark red; Sapphire, lavender-blue; Creole, light yellow; and May Queen, soft lilac. Mathiola bicornis, Night-scented Stock, valued for its fragrance rather than for its single lilac flowers, expands in the early evening like Nicotiana.

As with Salpiglossis, a well-grown planting of Stocks is an achievement for most amateurs. Oftentimes there are many "blind" plants which refuse to bloom, producing great masses of foliage instead. It is known that Stocks must be kept in active growth from the time the seed is sown until they bloom. Start the seed in a coldframe or in the open ground, and transplant the seedlings as soon as they have produced four or six leaves. Young plants should not be allowed to become rootbound in pots or flats. Stocks grow best in a cool, moist temperature where the soil is rich in available plant-food. Water the plants freely, especially during dry spells, and grow them in full sun.

## MESEMBRYANTHEMUM (me-sem-bre-an'thee-mum).
### Fig-Marigold; Iceplant

These six syllables mean "mid-day flower," in reference to the fact that the blossoms expand only on sunny days. (The name is no harder to say than "chrysanthemum.") Curiously enough, one species (Mesembryanthemum crystallinum) of this large genus from South Africa is known as Iceplant because of the tiny globules which form on the leaves. For a hot, sandy location, M. crystallinum, with its strange foliage and small daisy-

like pink flowers, is worth growing. Then there is the Livingstone
Daisy, M. criniflorum, which is noted for its compact growth and
free-flowering habit. Both species are good summer material
for sun-baked areas in the rock-garden.

Sow the seed in the open ground and set the plants two to four inches
apart in a sunny location.

## MIMULUS (mim'you-lus). MONKEY-FLOWER

Monkey-Flower is the name usually applied to this genus
which bears the Latin name meaning "mimic"—a reference to
the curious, spotted flowers which look like ridiculous grimaces.
Along the West Coast, where they are native, many of the
species are perennials, but in eastern gardens they are treated as
annuals. Mimulus moschatus is known as Musk-Plant because
of the musk-like odor of its foliage. The yellow, tubular flowers
are spotted brown and reddish brown. Its creeping habit suggests its use for foreground planting. M. tigrinus, the true
Monkey-Flower, is easily distinguished by its gloxinia-like
flowers, which are curiously marked and spotted. Usually the
seed comes in mixture, including shades of pink, red, and yellow.

Sow seed of both species in a sunny window or coldframe, and set the
plants at least six inches apart. Mimulus grows well in moist, shady places,
and the plants are often grown in pots. M. tigrinus is by nature a tender
perennial, and needs to be started in February.

## MIRABILIS (mi-rab'bil-is). FOUR-O'CLOCK

John Parkinson, that great English gardener of the seventeenth century, wrote with great enthusiasm about the Four-
o'Clock (Mirabilis Jalapa) which he knew as the Marvel of Peru,
as some seedsmen yet call it. In our day it has been regrettably
neglected. Often it grows three feet or more in height, producing
strong, bushy plants which flower in the late afternoon, and remain in bloom until the warmth of the sun strikes them on the
following morning. Planted near buildings, it provides a desirable effect in the way of temporary foundation planting, in
addition to a source of rich fragrance which fills the air.

The seed may be sown in the open in early spring and the resulting
tubers dug in the autumn and stored as one would dahlias. Set the plants

fifteen inches apart in full sun. In its native habitat this plant is perennial, and in the warm regions of our country it may be treated as such.

MORNING-GLORY. See Ipomœa, page 55.

## MYOSOTIS (my-o-so'tis). FORGET-ME-NOT

For many garden enthusiasts, Forget-Me-Nots have a sentimental appeal akin to that of pansies. This association traces back to the time when the language of flowers was a popular fad. Each flower had its symbolism, and bouquets were arranged to convey messages. The Forget-Me-Not was a symbol of remembrance. Myosotis is the Greek equivalent for "mouse ear," a reference to the soft, hairy leaves.

Perhaps Forget-Me-Nots do not belong in a book of annuals, because they are classed as biennials and perennials, yet the varieties most commonly grown are treated as hardy annuals, like pansies. Both plants often self-sow in the same way. These forms of Myosotis alpestris need winter protection: Alba, white; Lavender Gem, a distinct lavender tint; Messidor, with its dark blue flowers; Rosea, a good pink kind; Royal Blue; and Victoria, with its azure blooms. As a ground-cover for shady areas, or for interplanting with spring bulbs, or even as edging plants, Forget-Me-Nots have their valuable place.

Sow the seed in midsummer (August 15 to September 1, according to your locality). The plants need winter protection, and are best set in raised beds, allowing six inches between plants, or in coldframes. A winter covering of hay or straw is the simplest protective cover.

NASTURTIUM. See Tropæolum, page 88.

## NEMESIA (ne-mee'she-a). NEMESIA

Surely the old doctor Dioscorides never knew the infinite variety of colors that we enjoy today in the hybrid Nemesias! Yet some botanist of a later generation attached this scientific name (found in the writings of Dioscorides) to these delightful flowers. A tender annual native to South Africa, it grows abundantly in England where it has been widely hybridized. Nemesia makes a colorful effect when planted in solid beds or in irregular "drifts" with other annuals. As a cut-flower, it offers unusual

PETUNIA, MARTHA WASHINGTON
*See page 72*

PETUNIA, SNOWSTORM
*See page 73*

possibilities for color combinations. Compact in its habit of growth, the plant is seldom more than a foot tall. It thrives in areas where the summers are cool.

Start the seed in a coldframe or in the open ground, and set the plants six inches apart in full sun. They grow best in rich soil.

## NEMOPHILA (ne-mof'i-la). NEMOPHILA

Many of the delightful California wild flowers are adaptable to the gardens of the eastern United States, but few of them are widely grown. One of the daintiest is Nemophila, which means "grove-loving," a characteristic of some species of the genus. The plants seldom grow more than a foot high, and the blue cup-

shaped blossoms of Nemophila insignis are not unlike those of
hardy flax. They are known as Baby Blue-Eyes.

Sow the seed in the open ground and space the plants four inches apart.
Make several sowings for a succession of bloom.

## NICOTIANA (ni-ko-she-ay'na). FLOWERING TOBACCO

Fragrance gives that indefinable quality of atmosphere to
every garden, however small, and this fact is reason enough for
growing Nicotiana. This genus name commemorates Jean Nicot,
a French ambassador who introduced tobacco (to smoke!) to
Queen Catherine de Medici in the sixteenth century.

Although somewhat ragged in appearance during the heat of
the day, Nicotiana takes on a stately grandeur from late afternoon (when its fragrance is emitted) until early morning—a
period when gardens are most enjoyable. If the flowers are cut
when the petals are expanded, they will remain open in water.
Flowering Tobacco grows well in full sun or partial shade.

The hybrids of Nicotiana affinis, and more particularly those
strains with red flowers (N. Sanderæ) in combination with the
white forms, are very pleasing. The plants often grow three feet
tall and make a widespreading mass. A compact variety known
as Crimson Bedder grows fifteen inches tall, and there is a delightful white form listed as Snowstorm. (See illustration on page 55.)

Sow the seed in a coldframe or in the open ground, and allow the young
plants ample space in which to develop—at least eighteen inches each way.

## NIEREMBERGIA (near-em-ber'je-a). DWARF CUP-FLOWER

All too often beginners in the hobby of gardening are either
startled, amused, or discouraged by the plant names they encounter in seed catalogues and garden books. Yet, there is little
that the average amateur can do about nomenclature, since it
is, for the most part, the business of the botanists whose taxo-
nomic methods are often difficult to comprehend.

To be sure, Nierembergia hippomanica is a "mouthful" for
any red-blooded American, but it is also a plant of unusual and
delicate beauty. (This species may sometime bear its correct
name, N. cærulea.) Named for a Spanish Jesuit, the genus,

[ 67 ]

which is found in South America, includes the miniature rock-garden species, N. rivularis, a perennial known as White-Cup. The lavender-blue blossoms of N. hippomanica look like shallow chalices with golden centers. Seldom more than six inches tall, the compact plants make stream-lined mounds, and are known for their free-flowering habit. In those sections of our country where the summers are cool, it promises to be of value.

Start the seed in a sunny window or a greenhouse during February or early March. Set the plants six inches apart in full sun, and if possible in rich soil. It takes nearly four months to produce flowering plants from seed.

## NIGELLA (ny-jell'a). LOVE-IN-A-MIST

A meaningless name for one of our daintiest annuals, Nigella means black—an allusion to the color of the seeds. In the vernacular this plant has fared better, for it has such local names as Love-in-a-Mist, Lady-in-the-Bower, and even Devil-in-the-Bush. (It's a wonder no one has ever called it Moses-in-the-Bulrushes!)

While not a showy garden plant, Nigella is a most exquisite cut-flower. The lacy, asparagus-like foliage forms a loose halo around the delicately chiseled flowers which are poised on twelve-inch stems. It is significant that the most popular variety, a delightful cornflower-blue, bears the name of the late Miss Jekyll, England's most distinguished woman gardener of the last generation. A white form is sometimes grown.

Sow the seed in the open ground and thin the plants four to six inches apart in full sun. For a succession of bloom make several plantings. This annual often self-sows.

PANSY. See Viola, page 93.

## PAPAVER (pap'a-ver). POPPY

Long before Flanders Field had any significance for us, Poppies were favorite plants in American gardens. They have been cultivated for many centuries, primarily as a source of opium rather than for their intrinsic beauty. Few plants have held a greater or more mysterious fascination for men than the annual species, Papaver somniferum, from which this powerful drug is obtained. It is also the source of many outstanding garden hybrids. These and many other kinds flaunt their flamboyant beauty in our gardens without requiring any special care.

Poppies are most effective in broad masses, whether in mixture or in separate varieties. Many gardeners grow them in separate beds; thus it is possible to pull them out after flowering and replant the area with such fall-blooming annuals as marigolds or China asters. After the first year, Poppies tend to find their own places in the garden.

Papaver Rhœas, the Corn Poppy of Europe, is the source of the delightful Shirley varieties, including single and double forms. American Legion and Flanders Field are single forms with orange-scarlet flowers. Cavalcade, a Begonia-flowered type, has double scarlet blooms. In addition, several shades of pink, white, apricot, and grayish blue are listed by seedsmen.

Among the hybrids of the Opium Poppy, P. somniferum, are the following: Admiral, a single peony-flowered variety with white flowers, banded scarlet; Charles Darwin, a rich dark purple accentuated with black markings at the base of each petal; Dainty Lady, a rosy mauve shade with dark markings; Danebrog or Danish Flag, scarlet with white markings; King Edward, noted for its scarlet-red blooms; The Bride, a pure white form.

The double forms include Carnation-flowered and Peony-flowered varieties with a wide color-range, and named varieties as well. Cardinal, with its fringed flowers of rich cardinal-red; Mikado, a white form with blooms tipped scarlet; and White Swan, a pure white, fringed form, are a few of those listed by American seedsmen. The Tulip Poppy, P. glaucum, has great scarlet cup-shaped blooms which strongly resemble tulips.

Poppy seed may be sown in the fall for early flowering, followed by successive sowings for midsummer bloom. Mix the tiny seed with sand or finely sifted loam for more even distribution, and scatter it lightly. Care is needed in covering the seed, and a fine spray of water helps to settle it. Light brushwood or chicken wire helps to keep cats, dogs, and other pests from disturbing the soil until the seed has germinated. Since Poppies are not generally transplanted with ease by most amateurs, eliminate the weaker seedlings and allow nine to twelve inches between plants. A sunny location produces the best results. While the largest flowers are grown on rich soil, Poppies grow well under ordinary conditions. Once established, they return each year; in fact, self-sown plants are unusually vigorous.

PETUNIA (pee-toon′i-a). PETUNIA

In recent years American gardeners have become Petunia-conscious. It is significant that these popular bedding plants have been recognized with many awards in the All-America Selections. During the year 1937, Pennsylvania State College tested 426 varieties, collected from seed-houses throughout the world. As one would expect, there were many duplications because of the existing confused nomenclature. The name Petunia comes from South America, where the plant grows naturally, and is reported to be a local name for tobacco.

Few flowers are more widely used in parks and gardens, and this familiar annual may well be called the "window-box plant of America." There are few soils where Petunias will not grow abundantly. A sunny location suits them best, but they will grow satisfactorily in partial shade. For masses, large or small, they are effective. Blooming with unlimited freedom, they adapt themselves to formal and informal gardens.

Some are single, some are ruffled, and some are double and semi-double. All tend to be bushy in form, but some are more prostrate than others (especially the Balcony varieties), and still others are decidedly compact. An infinite variety of rose and blue shades, with rich velvety tones of purple and dark reddish violet, in addition to pale yellow and pure white, are the dominant colors.

In classifying Petunias according to their habits and uses, it seems natural to consider the common hybrid type first. These bloom profusely, reseed themselves freely, and grow about eighteen inches high. The most brilliant mixtures and a wide color-range are found in this class, as represented by General Dodds, noted for its ox-blood-red blooms; Howard's Star Improved, with its striking white star accentuating the deep purple flower; and Rose King Improved.

Medium-sized flowers on more compact and erect-growing plants, averaging twelve inches in height, give us a desirable bedding group. Rosy Morn, with its white throat; Rose of Heaven, Celestial Rose (illustrated on page 1), Blue Bedder, Salmon Supreme, and Snowball are typical varieties in this most

DRUMMOND PHLO
See page 74

RUDBECKIA, KELVEDON STAR
*See page 76*

useful class. Martha Washington (illustrated on page 65) is even more compact and dwarf, a delightful lavender-pink ruffled flower, with wine-red veins extending into a large violet throat.

A new strain of dwarf, compact, miniature Petunias is receiving praiseworthy attention. Brilliant Rose Gem is the most outstanding representative. The little ball-shaped plants, six to eight inches in height, are admirably adapted for edging, bedding, window-box, and pot-culture.

More pendulous in habit are the large-flowered Balcony Petunias, a glorified hybrid type. In addition to white, rose, crimson, and blue, there are named varieties like Black Prince, a velvety red, and Netted Blue Gem, a steel-blue tone.

As plant-types are divided, so also the flower formations are grouped. The large-flowering single varieties, like Elk's Pride, of rich violet, and Snowstorm (illustrated on page 66), are plain petaled, usually called P. grandiflora. Then there are the large-flowered single fringed sorts frequently called Fluffy Ruffles, including the popular golden-centered rose-pink Theodosia and pale yellow Dainty Lady. Those with large, veined throats are called Ruffled Giants. In the dwarf fringed group are the brilliant rose Setting Sun and the pure white Lace Veil.

The Giants of California strain is the largest flowered of all Petunias. Both the tall kinds, often eighteen inches high, and the dwarf types are free flowering, with huge veined throats in heavily textured ruffled flowers. Double and semi-double blooms in this gigantic-flowered strain may likewise be obtained in tall and dwarf plant forms, and varieties in separate colors are available. A word of caution is advisable here: the seed of these giant double Petunias is very expensive, and strains of any value cannot be purchased cheaply.

Petunias are tender perennials usually treated as hardy garden annuals, and seed germinates in about ten days. Sow the seed in a light soil mixture in pots or flats indoors during February or early March or in a coldframe. Mix the tiny seed with sand and press it into firm soil, covering it very lightly. Transplant the seedlings as soon as they are large enough to handle. When setting them out, allow twelve to fifteen inches between plants and give them a sunny location. Seed may be sown outdoors, but high-priced seed deserves more care and protection than is possible in the open.

## PHACELIA (fa-see′li-a). PHACELIA

A little-known annual, Phacelia is one of those California natives that need to be grown in more gardens. Its Greek name, meaning "cluster," relates to the arrangement of the blossoms. Both the pleasing blue tone of the shallow, cup-shaped flowers and the locality of its native home are conveyed in the name California Bluebell. Phacelia campanularia is perhaps the most familiar species; a free-flowering plant of compact habit, it bears its large, blue, campanula-like blossoms on compact plants seldom more than ten to twelve inches high. Then there is P. ciliata, with its fragrant lavender-blue flowers, which grows slightly taller, and P. viscida, a gentian-blue form with pale blue centers. These are plants for edgings or planting with other annuals in masses as well as for the rock-garden.

Sow the seed in a coldframe or in the open ground, and set the plants four to six inches apart in a sunny location. Light rich soil suits them best.

## PHLOX (flocks). PHLOX

An American plant with a Greek name meaning "flame," Phlox Drummondi remained an untamed wilding of the Southwest for more than two hundred years after the first American garden was planted. In 1835 an Englishman named Drummond collected seed in Texas and sent it to England! Such has been the history of many garden plants now in cultivation; almost invariably garden enthusiasts have neglected the native material of their respective localities, turning their attention first to exotic material, only to realize at some later time the beauty of their own wayside flowers.

The vivid centers or "eyes" of the individual florets accentuate the tints and shades of the many colors. (See illustration on page 71.) Among them are Brilliant, a rich crimson; Carmine; Chamois-Rose, a soft pink; Isabellina, light yellow; Kermesina, a scarlet-striped kind; Leopoldi, rose with a white eye; Purple King; and White. Gigantea Art Shades is an unusually large-flowered strain composed of many delightful pastel hues. A variety with star-shaped flowers of wide color-range is usually listed as Star of Quedlinburg, or Star Phlox. The dwarf form of Annual Phlox makes a showy border plant for annual or perennial gardens and shrub borders.

Start the seed in a coldframe or in the open ground and set the plants nine to twelve inches apart in full sun. Remove the seed-pods, and the plants will flower freely until killed by frost.

POPPY. See Papaver, page 68.

## PORTULACA (por-tew-lack'a). PORTULACA

This Brazilian native may well be considered an easy annual for everybody's garden, since it needs only a hot, sunny location and grows freely in any kind of soil. Its Latin name means "purslane" (pussley), to which it is related. Sun-Rose, Sun-Plant, Wax-Pink, and Rose-Moss are some of its many common names. An ideal ground-cover for hot, dry areas, it blooms incessantly, and requires no care except for weeding. Plant Portulaca where grass is difficult to grow. It has been used to advantage in driveways, between and along the sides of paved areas. Single- and double-flowering kinds are obtainable in many colors.

Scatter the seed broadcast and press it in lightly with a board. It self-sows frequently.

## RESEDA (re-zee'da). MIGNONETTE

Mignonette, like a breath of fragrance from an old Continental parlor, recalls the quaint gardens of the nineteenth century, in which fragrant flowers were more important than they are today. The Latin name of this North African plant means "I calm," an allusion to its supposed healing power for bruises. Hardly a penetrating fragrance, it may well be described as a delicate scent which adds materially to bouquets.

Several improved varieties are available: Goliath, a giant red-flowered kind; Machet, a dwarf variety; and Golden Queen, a yellow form, are all worth considering, as are other special strains which individual seedsmen feature. All are of subdued coloring.

Because it does not transplant easily, sow the seed in the open ground and thin the plants to a distance of six to nine inches. Several sowings are necessary for a succession of bloom, and it is best planted in the cutting garden in beds. It will grow satisfactorily in partial shade.

## RICINUS (ris'i-nus). CASTOR-BEAN

A rather coarse-growing curiosity, the Castor-Bean from tropical Africa is hardly suitable for the average garden. Ricinus is the Latin word for "tick"—a reference to the appearance of the seed. Its common name indicates that it is a source of castor-oil. While some of the plants are not more than three feet tall, others grow twelve feet, spreading their great palmate

[ 75 ]

leaves over a large area. There are several varieties: Ricinus communis cambodgensis, with bronzy foliage of medium height; Duchess of Edinburgh, with dark red foliage; and R. communis sanguineus, with red spots.

If you feel that you must grow this annual, sow the seed outside and allow the plants ample room to develop.

## RUDBECKIA (rood-beck′i-a). CONEFLOWER

A Swedish professor's name is attached to this genus. While some of the species are looked on as troublesome weeds, because both the untamed and the cultivated species self-sow readily, yet they contribute largely to the color of the midsummer garden, enduring hot, dry weather and providing quantities of cut-flowers.

These annual varieties of Rudbeckia will grow well in the shrub border, or they may be associated with perennials. As accentuating masses in the annual garden they fit well in the middle-ground planting. The mahogany and dark brown markings of R. bicolor distinguish it from R. hirta. Kelvedon Star (see illustration on page 72) is a vigorous plant often two and one-half feet tall, with striking flowers of brilliant orange-yellow, in contrast to the dark brown centers and mahogany zone. My Joy is noted for its extremely large flowers of bright orange.

Sow the seed in a coldframe or in the open ground, and set the plants at least fifteen to eighteen inches apart in full sun. Ordinary soil suits them.

## SALPIGLOSSIS (sal-pi-gloss′is). SALPIGLOSSIS

An aristocrat of the plant kingdom is the dainty Salpiglossis, which came to us originally from South America. It is sometimes called Painted-Tongue. In its color-range, form, and even in its requirements, this flower is in a class apart. Indeed, a well-grown bed of Salpiglossis is an achievement for any amateur. Poised in loose clusters, the tubular blossoms, which are not unlike Petunias in form, stand erect on two-and-one-half-foot stems. They are rich in tones of maroon, purple, and golden yellow, and other closely related shades. A dwarf strain is available also. (See illustration on page 77.)

Start the seed in a coldframe or in the open ground (in regions where the spring season is not too late). Since the plants are sparse of foliage, they

SALPIGLOSSIS HYBRIDS
*See page 76*

should be set six to nine inches apart. A sunny location and rich soil suit them best. The seedlings are weak and spindly in the young stage, and will benefit by applications of liquid manure. It may be necessary to stake the tall-growing type if they are not grown in a sheltered location. Pinch the young plants to make them branch.

## SALVIA (sal'vi-a). SAGE

Recognizing the medicinal value of the Garden Sage, Salvia officinalis, some early botanist named the genus Salvia, meaning

SCABIOSA HYBRIDS
*See page 80*

"to heal." When Salvia is mentioned, invariably many gardeners think of the brilliant Scarlet Sage (S. splendens) which has been misused to the point of abuse in many gardens, especially when grown near pink or purple Petunias. Let us use this Brazilian native with restraint, and plant more of the Mealy-cup Sage, S. farinacea, which grows naturally in Texas. Then there is S. Horminum from southern Europe, sometimes called Clary (true Clary is S. Sclarea) or Joseph Sage.

Scarlet Sage may be used effectively in the foreground of shrub borders or with perennials, provided it does not clash with the pink and purple tones of other flowers. Many varieties are offered, among which are: America, or Globe of Fire, noted for its compact growth habit, seldom over two feet; Blaze of Fire, a new dwarf variety; Bonfire; Harbinger, an early-blooming dwarf sort; Ostrich Plume, with its feather-like spikes; and Zurich. The introduction of the salmon-pink variety Welwyn, and a companion form with white flowers, suggests a wider use of this showy annual. There is little to recommend the purple form.

Mealycup Sage, S. farinacea, is an outstanding species with long racemes of lavender-blue flowers on graceful stems, with soft grayish foliage. A tender perennial form in Texas, this plant is commonly grown as an annual. Blue Bedder is an improved strain, of compact growth and free-flowering habit. An excellent plant for accentuating masses in the perennial border, it is equally valuable in the annual garden for background effects. There are few more desirable cut-flowers.

A compact annual species is the Joseph Sage, S. Horminum. It seldom grows more than eighteen inches tall and the pale lavender flowers would be of little consequence were it not for the showy violet bracts which enclose them.

All the Salvias, with the exception of S. Horminum, should be started indoors in February or early March. S. splendens is slow in germinating, and care must be taken not to water-soak the soil. Transplant the seedlings into a flat or coldframe. In the garden the plants need at least twelve to fifteen inches of space. Full sun and rich soil suit them best.

## SANVITALIA (san-vi-tal'i-a). SANVITALIA

Of Mexican origin, Sanvitalia procumbens, named for an Italian family of royalty, might well be called a miniature Zinnia. Although many seedsmen list it in their catalogues, it is not generally grown. Many garden enthusiasts complain of hot, dry areas which support little or no vegetation because of the extremely dry soil. This Creeping Zinnia (as it is sometimes called) is admirably suited to warm situations, and may be used as an annual ground-cover. The tiny, button-like, double golden yellow flowers, which are produced freely over a long period, are effective for miniature bouquets.

Start the seed in a coldframe or in the open ground, and thin or set the plants six inches apart.

## SCABIOSA (skay-be-oh'sa). SWEET SCABIOUS

Sweet Scabious, Pincushion-Flower, and Mourning Bride are the most commonly used names for this fine annual. The genus name is the Latin word for "itch" and was originally given to the common European species, which was considered a remedy for skin irritations. The common name Pincushion-Flower is a most appropriate description of the bloom, which is formed like an old-time pincushion. Undoubtedly the name Mourning Bride was attached because of the intense dark coloring found in the variety King of the Blacks—one of the darkest colors in garden flowers. (See illustration on page 78.)

The free-flowering habit, the showy blooms on long, slender stems, and the wide variety of its colors have made Scabiosa a very desirable plant and cut-flower. Lavender, several shades of pink, red, yellow, and white kinds, in addition to named varieties like Blue Cockade, Peach Blossom, Azure Fairy, and Rosette, are widely grown. Scabiosas are ideal plants for middle-ground planting in the annual or perennial border, and they bloom freely.

Sow the seeds in a coldframe or in the open ground, and set the plants six to nine inches apart in full sun. They will grow satisfactorily in partial shade and do not seem particular as to soil.

## SCHIZANTHUS (sky-zan'thus). BUTTERFLY-FLOWER

Any garden lover who has seen well-grown specimens of Schizanthus at the flower shows cannot but cherish the desire to grow this plant. But, alas, its delicate structure cannot easily resist the strong winds, the hot sun, or the beating rain, wherefore it is a plant for careful gardeners and those who have protecting greenhouses. The Greek name Schizanthus means "cut flower," alluding to the delicately fringed blooms which resemble the edging of old Irish lace. The more familiar names are Poor Man's Orchid and Butterfly-Flower. Few annuals are more decorative for flower arrangements.

If satisfied with small sprays of bloom, sow the seed in the open ground, mixing it with fine sand to secure even distribution. Since it is not readily transplanted, thin the seedlings to stand six to nine inches apart. Pinch out the centers of the young plants to make them bushy, and give them a sheltered location in partial shade. The plants come into flower quickly (five to six weeks). For a succession of bloom make several sowings.

SNAPDRAGON. See Antirrhinum, page 20.

STATICE (stat'i-see or stat'iss). SEA-LAVENDER

A Latin word meaning "stop," in allusion to its astringent qualities, Statice is commonly known as Sea-Lavender. The perennial species, as well as the annual kinds, are often combined with other everlastings for winter bouquets.

Three annual species are generally grown. Statice sinuata is most commonly seen, with its eighteen-inch stems which rise from compact masses of foliage. The individual flowers, in shades of mauve, rose, blue, and white, come in rows on short, angular stems. Statice Bonduelli is similar in appearance, but its flowers are yellow. The showiest kind of all is S. Suworowi, with long spikes (resembling cat-tails) of light pink flowers, closely set on slender but sturdy stems. It makes a colorful display in the garden and is most desirable for cutting.

Sow the seed in a coldframe or in the open ground, and set the plants nine to twelve inches apart in a sunny location. S. Suworowi is the only species that will lend a dominant color-note to gardens; hence the other species are best grown in rows in the cutting garden.

STOCK. See Mathiola, page 61.

SUNFLOWER. See Helianthus, page 52.

SWEET PEA. See Lathyrus, page 58.

TAGETES (tay-gee'teez). MARIGOLD

The African and French Marigolds that bloom so abundantly from midsummer to frost are of Mexican origin. Probably the story recorded by John Gerard in 1597 accounts for the name "African" Marigold. He told of its introduction to England by Charles V after the battle of Tunis. The French types were first introduced into the gardens of France. The name Marigold, originally attached to Calendula officinalis in honor of the Virgin Mary, has been commonly associated with several yellow flowers. Tagetes is the Latin name for an Etruscan god.

With the wide variations in height, color, and form it is possible to use these "hard-luck" annuals in many parts of the garden. The African varieties, for background planting, average two and one-half to three feet or more in height; the French forms, for the middle ground, grow from nine inches to two and one-half feet; the dwarf T. signata pumila, for edging purposes or pot-culture, grows nine to twelve inches tall.

Marigolds, like Zinnias, have attracted the attention of the hybridizers, with the result that, among the African types, we now have odorless kinds, one of which is known as Crown of Gold. The center petals of the orange flowers are curled and twisted, forming a high crown, surrounded by a row of somewhat drooping, flat guard-petals. Then there are the Dixie or Chrysanthemum-flowered hybrids (see illustration on page 43) with well-formed flowers, curiously incurved and quilled; these are available in orange, gold, and yellow shades. Dixie Sunshine, a yellow Chrysanthemum-flowered type of distinct pyramidal habit, requires a long period of growth before flowering, and is best adapted to the gardens of the South and Southwest. (An early-flowering form will undoubtedly be provided soon.) Guinea Gold well describes the gleaming orange-gold blooms of an excellent variety with looser and flatter form than the older types. Yellow Supreme (see illustration on page 44) is in many respects the yellow counterpart of Carnation-flowered Guinea Gold. All of these hybrids have come to our gardens as the result of the All-America Selections. Many seedsmen list other desirable varieties, including a dwarf African strain approximately eighteen inches tall.

Double and single forms are found among the French Marigolds, which also include tall and dwarf kinds. Among the tall

SWEET PEA, SHIRLEY TEMPLE
*See page 58*

TITHONIA, FIREBALL
*See page 87*

varieties separate colors are available of both single and double flowers. As with many annuals, the great variations in color are most easily realized by planting packets of mixed seed. Josephine, a tall single kind, is the variety most commonly grown. The velvety blooms are a combination of dark brown, red, and gold, and are supported by long, slender stems.

Many named varieties appear among the dwarf French Marigolds, which average twelve to fifteen inches in height. Dwarf Royal Scot is golden yellow with mahogany stripes. Harmony (see illustration on page 49) has a crested orange center, accentuated by maroon petals. Legion of Honor, sometimes called Little Brownie, is often less than a foot high; each yellow

petal of the flower is marked with a blotch of crimson. Of all the
dwarf Marigolds, none is more free-flowering or more delightful
than the so-called miniature variety, Tagetes signata pumila.
The delicately cut foliage is hardly noticeable because of the
profuse flowering habit of the yellow and orange forms.

Marigold seed may be sown in a sunny window, in a coldframe, or in the
open ground. The African and tall French varieties need ample space for
development; allow eighteen to twenty-four inches between the seedlings.
Most of the dwarf French types may be set twelve to fifteen inches apart,

VERBENA, LAVENDER GLORY
*See page 90*

ZINNIA, FANTASY STRAIN
*See page 95*

but Tagetes signata pumila needs to be spaced six inches apart. Marigolds are essentially sun-loving plants thriving in hot, dry areas without any particular soil-requirements.

## THUNBERGIA (thun-ber'ji-a). THUNBERGIA

Among the brightest of the trailing plants is the cheery Thunbergia alata, from tropical Africa, named for that great Swedish botanist whose name is associated with several familiar garden plants. It is sometimes called Black-eyed Susan, a name which more properly belongs to Rudbeckia hirta. Although a perennial in its native habitat, it is grown as an annual in eastern United States. For those garden enthusiasts limited to window-boxes, terrace gardens, or roof-gardens, Thunbergia is a plant to lend variety to the usual vines, Petunias, Alyssum, Lobelia, and the familiar red Geranium. The buff-colored flowers, nearly an inch in diameter, are marked with dark centers. Shades of orange and yellow are also available.

Start the seed indoors in late February and set the plants out when all danger of frost has passed. Many florists grow this plant, and it is usually possible to buy small seedlings ready to transplant.

## TITHONIA (ti-tho'ni-a). TITHONIA

As brilliant as the pottery of its native land is the sturdy and tall-growing Mexican Sunflower, Tithonia rotundifolia or speciosa. This genus is named for Tithonus, a mythological character beloved of Aurora. It no doubt had a place in the gardens of the ancient Inca civilization, since it is known as the Golden Flower of the Incas. While hardly a plant for a small garden, since it often grows twelve feet or more in height (especially during moist summers), it is an entertaining curiosity. The large, coarse foliage resembles that of a fig or mulberry tree, and the showy flowers, like single Dahlias, are often three to four inches across, and brilliant vermilion. The variety Fireball is a dazzling orange-scarlet. (See illustration on page 84.)

Start the seed early (January or early February if possible) because the plants require a long period to develop. Set them three to four feet apart, in full sun, and hope for maturity before frost. An abundance of moisture seems to stimulate foliage growth rather than flowers.

## TORENIA (tor-ren'i-a). TORENIA

It was a Swedish clergyman and botanist who discovered this valuable little annual in China, in 1750, and for him it is named. Had this plant been known in England a century earlier, undoubtedly it would have been considered of great medicinal value because of the noticeable wishbone form which the stamens assume. Surely old Nicholas Culpepper, the seventeenth-century herbalist, would have found some application of the curious doctrine of signatures in this unusual flower!

Torenia is a refined plant, with rich dark green foliage and dainty snapdragon-like flowers, that grows well in shady areas and blooms profusely. The blossoms of T. Fournieri are lavender-blue, combined with rich purple, and further accentuated by a golden yellow blotch on the lower lip. T. Bailloni (flava), a bright yellow species with a purplish throat, is not as commonly grown, but it makes a fine companion for T. Fournieri.

It is best to sow the seed in a greenhouse or coldframe and when all frost danger is past, set the plants outdoors at least six inches apart. Make use of this annual in some partially shaded corner of the garden.

## TROPÆOLUM (tro-pee'o-lum). NASTURTIUM

There is a homely beauty about the old-fashioned single Nasturtiums that can hardly be replaced by the modern double hybrids. This statement is not made to disparage the value of the improved varieties, which are a distinctive contribution to twentieth-century gardens, but rather to emphasize the fact that the old favorites should not be forgotten. Tropæolum, from the Greek, means "trophy," as associated with the shield-like form of the leaves. The familiar name Nasturtium signifies "that which twists the nose," a reference to the pungent leaves of some species.

Because Nasturtiums grow with such vigor, they are well suited for covering large areas, more especially unsightly places. The tall varieties are often trained on trellises, but they grow downward over banks and walls with greater ease. (Tropæolum canariensis, the Canary-bird-Vine, with its lacy yellow blossoms, makes a delightful vine for trellises, pergolas, and fences.)

Shades of scarlet, crimson, maroon, rose, salmon, yellow, and

white are found in the named varieties of Nasturtium and mixtures offered by most seedsmen. King Theodore has unusually
dark foliage and reddish brown flowers sometimes described as
maroon. Then there is Lobb's Mixture, developed from T.
Lobbianum, which is outstanding for its very large blossoms.

The semi-double Gleam Hybrids may well be described as
intermediate in height. For pot-culture they may be grown on
trellises, but in gardens they are best treated as trailing plants.
Golden Gleam, Orange Gleam, Scarlet Gleam, and other shades
are listed separately in catalogues; the Glorious Gleam mixture
includes many intermediate shades. (See illustration, page 50.)

The dwarf or Tom Thumb Nasturtiums are as varied in their
color-range as are the tall, single kinds. Golden Globe, Scarlet
Globe, and the Globe mixture produce their semi-double flowers
freely on compact plants averaging a foot in height.

It doesn't take a "green thumb" to grow Nasturtiums! Sow the seed
in the open ground as soon as the soil becomes warm. Since the individual
seeds are large enough to handle separately, they may be set fifteen inches
apart; the tall varieties are more vigorous and need twenty to twenty-four
inches between plants. Some gardeners start the seed indoors in pots, and
later transfer the plants to the garden. The young seedlings are tender and
do not transplant readily, but they may be moved with a ball of earth.
Full sun and poor soil are their meager requirements. The black lice often
found on the plants may be eradicated with a nicotine or pyrethrum spray.

## URSINIA (ur-sin′i-a). URSINIA

Jewel of the Veldt aptly describes this South African annual
of comparatively recent introduction, and, together with Venidium which follows, it is of rather difficult growth for the average
amateur. Our English neighbors are most enthusiastic about it
but their climate is not as variable as ours.

From tufts of delicately cut foliage the flower-stems of
Ursinia anethoides arise to a height of twelve inches, displaying
gay orange daisy-like flowers, marked with a zone of purplish
crimson near the dark centers. The variety Aurora is an improvement of the species growing eight inches tall, and U. pul-
chra is a dwarf form not more than six inches high.

Start seed of Ursinia in a coldframe in March and set the plants six to
nine inches apart in full sun where the soil is rich but well drained.

## VENIDIUM (ve-nid′i-um). VENIDIUM

A South African annual known as Monarch of the Veldt is Venidium fastuosum. This newcomer has flowers that are equally as spectacular as those of Ursinia. The plants are taller, and the individual bright orange blossoms are larger. But this annual is not of easy culture. Perhaps after it has been more widely grown, a strain adapted to our climate will be developed. The plants average two feet or more in height.

Start the seed in warm soil and set the plants in a sunny location at least a foot apart. Over-fertilized soil may produce imperfect flowers; keep it on the "poor" side as to soil, and if possible grow it in sandy loam.

## VERBENA (ver-bee′na). VERBENA

The name Verbena dates back to the writings of Pliny, and was applied to Verbena officinalis, the only European species. With this exception, all of the species are native in North and South America.

It is a comparatively simple matter to grow annuals in rows, as one would vegetables, but it takes a little more skill to combine them harmoniously in a well-planned garden. Hot, dry areas often constitute a problem in this respect. In such places, Verbenas become a part of the landscape.

Many separate colors are obtainable. Apple Blossom has dainty pink coloring, as its name suggests. The brilliant rose shades of the Beauty of Oxford hybrids are extraordinary. Dannebrog, with its striking scarlet blooms, was given an Award of Merit in the 1934 All-America Selections. Etna is a brilliant scarlet with a dainty yellow eye. Floradale Beauty, which is the result of selection from the Beauty of Oxford hybrids, was recognized in the 1937 All-America Selections. Then there is Lavender Glory (see illustration on page 85); Luminosa, with its salmon shades; Royale, a royal blue tone; Spectrum Red; White Giant; and Violet Bouquet. The new, compact, erect type, as represented by the variety Fireball, is only six inches tall.

Sow the seed in a coldframe or in the open ground and allow twelve to fifteen inches between plants. Put them in full sun and keep the seed-pods picked off. Some gardeners carry desirable varieties over winter in a cool greenhouse or window garden and propagate plants by cuttings.

POMPON ZINNIAS
*See page 95*

ZINNIA LINEARIS
*See page 95*

ZINNIA, CALIFORNIA GIANT TYPE
*See page 94*

[ 92 ]

## VINCA (vin'ka). PERIWINKLE

This name brings to mind that indispensable perennial ground-cover, Vinca minor, which is completely hardy and widely used. Then there is a variegated species, V. major variegata, also of trailing habit, commonly seen in window-boxes. Comparatively few gardeners grow the Madagascar Periwinkle, V. rosea, which is a tender perennial usually treated as an annual. A sunny exposure seems to be one of the few requirements of this showy plant, which usually grows about a foot high. In public parks and gardens the Madagascar Periwinkle is often grown as a bedding plant because of its rich foliage and showy flowers which are produced freely through the summer. The glossy foliage has noticeable veins, and the showy rose-colored flowers distinctive red centers. A white form with a rosy red eye is also available.

Start the seed indoors or in a coldframe, and set the plants six inches apart in a sunny place in the garden. Grow the plant in generous masses.

## VIOLA (vy-oh'la). PANSY

It is rather significant that the Johnny-jump-up, or Hearts-ease (as Viola tricolor is more familiarly known), is being featured now in the catalogues of many American seedsmen. For considerably more than two hundred years these sprightly faces have been bobbing up here and there in American gardens, unnoticed and neglected. Yet they have persisted, and are now introduced as Shakespeare's Pansies. Such they are, similar in form and color to the Heartsease used in Elizabethan tussie-mussies or nosegays. The name Viola is an old Latin term, and the common name Pansy is from the French, meaning "thoughts."

Surprising as it appears at first glance, the giant-flowered Pansies (Viola tricolor hortensis) of our twentieth-century gardens have been developed from the tiny Heartsease of Shakespeare's day. (See illustration on page 56.)

The Trimardeau strain is known for its medium-sized flowers and extraordinary color-range, including a number of separate colors. Then there are the present-day giant-flowering kinds: Roggli or Swiss Giants and their dwarf hybrids, the

# ANNUALS FOR YOUR GARDEN

Maple-Leaf Giants, the Non Plus Ultra Mixture, the Mastodon Pansies, the Masterpiece strain, the Orchid-flowered Pansies, and the many other special strains of the seedsmen.

Pansy seed may be started indoors or in a coldframe during February or early March for late summer and fall bloom. However, the most satisfactory results are obtained by sowing the seed in early August. Select a partially shaded location for the seed-bed, or use a coldframe. It is important to keep the seed-bed moist, because the summer heat and wind tend to dry out the soil quickly. In preparing the ground for the seedlings one should remember that Pansies need a soil rich in available plant-food. Use well-rotted cow-manure, sheep-manure, or commercial fertilizer (according to directions), digging it well into the ground; allow the fertilizer to become thoroughly integrated with the soil for several weeks before planting. Drainage is equally important; if the soil is essentially heavy, or if the area is low, raise the beds to a height of four inches above the surrounding ground. Set the seedlings four to six inches apart and give them occasional applications of liquid manure. If not carried over in a coldframe, the best winter protection is straw or hay, and it should not be put on until the ground has frozen hard. Many amateur gardeners complain that Pansies become "leggy" in late spring, and stop blooming. They fail to realize that it is essential to remove all seed-pods and cut back the "leggy" growth in order to keep the plants in a healthy condition.

## ZINNIA (zin'i-a). ZINNIA; YOUTH AND OLD AGE

Zinnias take their place of popularity in our gardens along with Asters, Marigolds, and Petunias. Although native to Mexico, this genus perpetuates the name of a German doctor of the eighteenth century. The name Youth and Old Age has been applied to them because one often sees partially faded flowers on the same plant with half-developed blooms.

A sufficiently great number of hybrids of varying sizes, forms, heights, and colors is available today to make an entire garden of Zinnias. Perhaps the most striking and certainly the most satisfactory of popular annuals are the Giant Dahlia-flowered Zinnias, the blooms of which sometimes exceed six inches in diameter and three inches in depth. Shades of scarlet, rose, orange, yellow, white and lavender are available in separate colors. Well-developed plants usually grow three feet tall. The so-called California Giants (see illustration, page 92) are distinguished for their large size, but they are flatter in form than the Dahlia-flowered types and are often preferred for cutting.

Then there are the Dwarf Double-flowering kinds, known as the "Cut-and-Come-Again" type, with flowers averaging about two inches in diameter, borne on plants eighteen inches tall.

Lilliput or Pompon Zinnias (see illustration, page 91) are very useful for cutting, and bloom profusely over a long period. Fifteen inches is usually their limit. The button Zinnia, Red Riding Hood, is decidedly miniature with its half-inch flowers borne on twelve-inch plants. Among the dwarf Zinnias the Tom Thumb mixture is distinguished for its four to six-inch plants.

Crown o' Gold is a new form of Zinnia—a variation of the giant-flowered type. Its claim to distinction is the golden yellow touch at the base of each petal.

Fantasy Zinnias are hybrids of the Quilled and Crested types. They produce medium-sized flowers with twisted petals on stems two to three feet tall, and are available in a variety of colors. (See illustration on page 86.)

Zinnia linearis is a recent introduction to American gardens. Usually it grows nine to twelve inches tall and has a tendency to semi-prostrate growth. The single flowers have dark centers. (See illustration on page 91.) It has great possibilities.

Mexican Zinnias (Z. Haageana) are valued for their rich mahogany shades and for the unique bicolor forms that occur in many of the recent hybrid mixtures.

Picotee Zinnias are vigorous-growing plants with medium-sized flowers. Delicate picotee edgings mark the tips of the petals.

Although the Quilled or Cactus Zinnias are by no means new to many garden lovers, new strains of these varieties have been offered by seedsmen in recent years.

The new Scabious-flowered Zinnias have crowned centers circumscribed by one or two rows of ray petals, and resemble the annual Scabiosa. Usually the plants grow about two feet tall.

Zinnias are so easily raised from seed that they are often among the first plants which beginners grow. Start the seed in a coldframe or in the open ground, and transplant the seedlings before they become spindly. When planting Zinnias in beds and borders, provide ample space for the development of the seedlings; usually the distance between plants should equal one-half of the height of the strain being grown. Although not particular as to soil, they thrive in rich loam, and full sun suits them best.

# INDEX